T0164999

Dwelling
in the
Land of Goshen

DENISE KELLEY

WestBow
PRESS
A DIVISION OF THOMAS NELSON

Copyright © 2012 by Denise Kelley.

All rights reserved. No part of this book may be used or reproduced by any means, graphic, electronic, or mechanical, including photocopying, recording, taping or by any information storage retrieval system without the written permission of the publisher except in the case of brief quotations embodied in critical articles and reviews.

Scripture references in this book are taken from the King James version of the Bible, unless otherwise noted

WestBow Press books may be ordered through booksellers or by contacting:

WestBow Press
A Division of Thomas Nelson
1663 Liberty Drive
Bloomington, IN 47403
www.westbowpress.com
1-(866) 928-1240

Because of the dynamic nature of the Internet, any web addresses or links contained in this book may have changed since publication and may no longer be valid. The views expressed in this work are solely those of the author and do not necessarily reflect the views of the publisher, and the publisher hereby disclaims any responsibility for them.

Any people depicted in stock imagery provided by Thinkstock are models, and such images are being used for illustrative purposes only.

Certain stock imagery © Thinkstock.

ISBN: 978-1-4497-4328-4 (hc)
ISBN: 978-1-4497-4326-0 (sc)
ISBN: 978-1-4497-4327-7 (e)

Library of Congress Control Number: 2012904611

Printed in the United States of America

WestBow Press rev. date: 04/19/2012

Table of Contents

To my loving husband, Joe. No one knows the miracle of our "dwelling in the land of Goshen" better than you do. We have known the heartache of living in Lodebar. I love you for being a mighty man of valor, courageous in all your ways, and I dedicate this literary work to you.

Denise and Joe Kelley

He that dwelleth in the secret place of the most High shall abide under the shadow of the Almighty.

(Psalm 91:1)

After our son Jonathan's death, life lost its meaning. Each morning brought dread and pain, and it was a daunting task just to get out of bed. More than anything, I wanted simply to not wake up. I dreaded every second, minute, and hour of every day and thought a lot about my own death. I lost all appreciation of life.

The thought that consumed and paralyzed me was I failed Jonathan. He was my responsibility. How is it that I allowed Jonathan to die? It had to be someone's fault; someone had to be blamed. It was my fault. What if I failed my other children? What had my husband and I done to deserve this? How could I have avoided this? The grief and sadness surrounding me was overwhelming. I spent a great deal of time at the cemetery during those first days after Jonathan's demise. I wanted—I *needed*—to be near Jonathan's body. It seemed my will, direction, and purpose were lost.

One day, while talking with my pastor, Gwendolyn Graham of Triumph Christian Center in Sugar Land, Texas, she said, "Write it down, Denise. Capture your feelings and thoughts in a journal." I remember thinking, *Write it all down? For what? I never want to remember or revisit the place where I am now or share these emotions with anyone.* I was very wrong that day. It has been almost ten years since Jonathan left us for heaven. In these ten years, my husband and I have experienced many lows—we expected that—but what has surprised us is that we have experienced a great many highs.

Many good things that we never thought possible have happened in our lives since then. We've learned so much, but the lesson that has meant the most is the promise God gave us from the start. Immediately after confirmation of Jonathan's death, we both heard the scripture "My grace is sufficient." It was God speaking to us. Reassuring us during a tragic time. God's word promises that his grace will abound much more . . . more than we can ask or expect.

Moreover, the law entered, that the offense might abound.
But where sin abounded, grace did much more abound:
Romans 5:20

All that passing laws against sin did was produce more lawbreakers.
But sin didn't, and doesn't, have a chance in competition with the
aggressive forgiveness we call grace. When it's sin versus grace, grace
wins hands down. All sin can do is threaten us with death, and that's
the end of it. Grace, because God is putting everything together again
through the Messiah, invites us into life—a life that goes on and on
and on, world without end.
Romans 5:20, 21 (The Message Bible)

His grace is whatever we need it to be—his grace is the light in the midst of total darkness. His grace is the comfort in the midst of excruciating pain. His grace is the relief valve when life's pressures seem about to blow the containment wall. God's grace provides us with the ability to choose life when it seems that the only practical choice is death.

God's Grace is Sufficient

A friend told me many years ago that I have the uncanny ability to see things as I want them to be, not as they really are. He was teasing me about my optimistic point of view. I always want to see the best in others, as well as in circumstances and situations. I want to believe that people's motives are pure. I realize this isn't always true, but I choose to believe in mankind's inner goodness; this is my chosen truth.

Sanctify them through thy truth: thy word is truth:
John 17:17

Truth is recorded in the written Word of God. We can choose either to believe God or not to believe God—those are the only two real choices in life. We all have been given the ability to choose, and this is my story of choices. The grace of God abounded in my life during very challenging times, and it is because of God's grace that our family is able to dwell in the land of Goshen. This is a story of God's extreme measures and love for his children. This is our family's true love story.

Acknowledgments

To my son, Joe Nathan Kelley II, and my daughters, Brittany Denise and Toni Johnson-Kelley—thank you. You are rocks, solid and unmovable in your love and strength for our family. I am so proud you call me Mom. I love you.

To my parents, Bishop John P. and evangelist Rebecca B. Worthy—thank you. I love you. You encourage me to live life every day, one day at a time. Your faith and prayers make me strong and persistent. When I think of giving up, I am reminded of your example of steadfast determination, and I make the choice to emulate you.

To my sisters, Viola Renee, La Donna Jean, Rebecca Alicia, and Nicole Renise, and my brother, Grady Earle—thank you. It seems that we have been through so much together as a family. One thing I am sure of is that "We Are Family." Through our disagreements and disappointments in one another, we have never, ever stopped being family, nor stopped being there for one another. Your love means everything to me. I love you all so much, and I am so proud you call me big sister.

To our grandchildren, Ashley, Halle, Kailyn, and Jonathan Bernard—thank you. I love you all so much and have such high hopes for your futures. I bless you in every endeavor of your life. I light up when you call me Grandma.

To my mother-in-law, Bessie Kelley—thank you. I love you. Your support is without end. Yours is the mother-in-law pattern I have fashioned for myself. I appreciate your steadfast ability to remain fair in the very challenging and difficult circumstances as Joe and I became one. I am so proud you call me daughter.

And last, to our middle son, Jonathan DeWitt Andrew Kelley—I love you still.

Joe II, Denise, Brittany and Joe Sr.

Our Family

Joe Sr., Brittany, Jonathan DeWitt Andrew, Denise and Joe II

And thou shalt dwell in the land of Goshen, and thou shalt be near unto me, thou, and thy children, and thy children's children, and thy flocks, and thy herds, and all that thou hast: And there will I nourish thee;

(Genesis 10, 11b)

INTRODUCTION

Genesis 45 is an example of the extreme measures to which God goes to ensure provision for his children who love and fear him. God is not surprised by any of life's events, circumstances, or situations, even when it seems like an unexpected calamity for us.

Beginning in Genesis 37, we see life's blank pages starting to record the journey of Joseph, the son of Jacob (later called Israel). Joseph, after many problems and unfair circumstances, acknowledges that God intended it all for his advantage. God loves Jacob and his family so much that he orchestrates life's circumstances and events to cause Joseph to be in the right place at the right time, so that supernatural increase, blessings, and favor can be poured on the children of Israel. Why would God do all this for these people? He did it so his people would be protected and provided for in due season.

And let us not be weary in well doing: for in due season we shall reap, if we faint not.
Galatians 6:9

God's grace abounded for his people then, and his grace abounds now. God is faithful, and he keeps his word. He was faithful yesterday, he is faithful today, and he will be faithful forever. God is as committed to his word today as he was when he spoke to Abraham.

The Beginning (Genesis 37)

Joseph was a dreamer. He was the second youngest of the twelve sons of Jacob (Israel). Joseph's father greatly loved him. Jacob gave Joseph a special gift, a coat of many colors, as a symbol of his love and affection. It was as if this gift to Joseph was the final straw for the older brothers. Their father's special love for Joseph became the focus of their hatred for their brother. They were jealous of Joseph and their father's special relationship.

Joseph often talked to his family about the things he saw in his dreams. The first of Joseph's dreams was of a sheaf of wheat that rose higher than those of his brothers; in fact, his brothers' sheaves bowed to Joseph's. The second dream was similar to the first, except this dream involved the sun, moon, and eleven stars, all of which bowed to Joseph. His father and brothers asked, "Shall we bow to you?" His brothers hated Joseph all the more because of his dreams and his words.

I have heard the adage, "God's favor is not fair," many times. When God blesses and ordains someone for a work, nothing can stop God's plan. None of us determines the state in which we begin our lives—good or bad, rich or poor, happy or not. As with Joseph, his father's favor was not Joseph's doing, but it was for his benefit—and that is why Joseph's brothers plotted to kill him. Had it not been for his eldest brother's intervention, the others surely would have carried out their plan, which was to kill Joseph and then tell their father that wild beasts had eaten him. Instead, they placed Joseph in a pit, sold him into slavery, and then dipped his colorful coat into blood as evidence for their father that Joseph had been killed. When the coat was brought to Jacob, he grieved for many days and would not be comforted.

> **We grow in favor daily with God and man**

Joseph's Challenges (Genesis 39)

Joseph began a long journey after his brothers sold him into slavery. The prophet Isaiah asked, "Will we believe God?" Joseph was taught his entire childhood of the goodness and saving grace of God the Father. It was the thread of knowledge to which he clung during times of excruciating hardship and

> **Believe God when there is no tangible or credible evidence**

anguish. Joseph decided he would believe God regarding his deliverance from captivity. While waiting for God's deliverance, Joseph would serve and work unto God. He decided to be the best he could be under the most extreme circumstances. No matter what situation Joseph found himself in, he wanted God to be glorified through him. It was a purposeful decision. Joseph determined that he would bloom wherever he was planted.

Joseph was taken to Egypt and sold to Potiphar, a captain of Pharaoh's army. It was a hard transition for Joseph to go from favored son to slave in a foreign land and household, but he remembered his father's teachings. Joseph held on to the report of the Lord—that the Lord God Jehovah will deliver. He knew the truth. He did not belong to himself; somehow, God would right the wrong. He knew of God's great love for his children and believed in the faithfulness of Lord God Jehovah, the great and mighty God. Joseph was committed to the knowledge of God's extreme love for him; therefore, Joseph trusted and believed in God. He believed in God, with no tangible or credible evidence. Joseph believed in God while enduring the hardships and burdens of his circumstance. He held onto his profession that God would rescue him.

Potiphar, a wealthy and shrewd businessman, quickly took notice of Joseph's abilities and noticed that others responded well to Joseph. Potiphar made Joseph the manager of his house and placed him in charge of all that he owned. Afterward, the Lord blessed Potiphar's house and possessions for Joseph's sake, and the blessing of God was upon all Potiphar owned. God rewarded Potiphar's kindness toward Joseph by blessing him even more.

> **Make the choice to obey and serve God everyday**

Joseph was a good man, and others thought well of him because of his goodness. As time progressed and Joseph matured in Potiphar's house, the master's wife noticed how beautiful Joseph had become. She found Joseph extremely appealing, and she desired him sexually. She propositioned Joseph, but he refused her. He reminded her that her husband trusted him with all he had. Joseph asked, "How could you expect me to do such a wicked thing against God?" His master's wife, however, would not accept no for an answer, and she badgered him day after day to be with her.

One day Joseph arrived at Potiphar's house to perform his normal duties, but Potiphar was away on business. Potiphar's wife grabbed Joseph and commanded that he sleep with her. Joseph ran, leaving his coat in her clenched hand. After this refusal, Potiphar's wife was extremely angry. She accused Joseph of trying to rape her and showed his coat as the proof. Once again, Joseph's coat was used as evidence against him. Potiphar, who believed his wife, had Joseph thrown in jail. Even in jail, however, the favor of God was with Joseph, and God showed favor toward him. The jail keeper liked Joseph and made him a trustee. God's favor remained with Joseph, and all he did was considered good.

Joseph's Prayer Request (Genesis 40)

One day, two new inmates entered the jail. They both served the king of Egypt. One was the king's baker and the other, his butler. Joseph was instructed to serve them. One morning while attending to them, Joseph noticed they were sadder than usual. He asked why their countenance was down. They told him they both had disturbing dreams the night before and did not know the meaning of their dreams. Joseph asked them, "Do not interpretations belong to God? Tell me your dreams."

After the butler and the baker each told Joseph his dream, Joseph told them the meanings of their dreams as God gave him revelation. He told the butler that in three days, he would be restored to his position and continue to serve the king. The baker, however, would not return to his past duties; he would be killed by the king. After interpreting the butler's dream, Joseph asked the butler to tell the king about him so that he could be released. Joseph told the butler about the unfairness of his situation and that he had been wrongly taken from his home and had done nothing wrong. The butler promised he would remember Joseph to the king.

In three days, just as Joseph had said, the baker was hanged and the butler was restored. The butler went back to his duties serving the king, but he forgot his promise to Joseph.

Joseph's Patience Rewarded (Genesis 41)

Two years after interpreting the dreams of the butler and the baker, the king had a dream. The king's dream bothered him, but he did not understand its meaning and desperately wanted an interpretation. He called for his advisors and told them the dream, but none could tell him its meaning.

God's promises are yes and amen

It was after much searching for an interpretation that the butler remembered Joseph's story. The butler told the king of his experience in jail and of Joseph's ability to tell the meaning of dreams.

A man's gift maketh room for him, and bringeth him before great men.
Proverbs 18:16

Pharaoh, the king of Egypt, sent for Joseph. The king told Joseph his dream. "There are actually two dreams." The King said to Joseph. "In the first I was standing near the Nile River and saw seven fat cows come from the Nile River. Then came seven thin cows. The seven thin cows consumed the seven fat cows but did not look any healthier as a result. Then I woke up." "I went back to sleep and had a second dream", explained the King. "In this dream there were seven wonderfully full and lush ears of grain growing from a single stalk. Then grew seven ears of grain that were thin and dried out. The seven thin ears swallowed up the full and lush ears. Then I woke up."

Joseph told Pharaoh the interpretation of the dream as God revealed it to him. Joseph explained to the king that dreams come from God to let us in on what he plans to do. The dreams had come to him twice because it had been established by God and would soon surely come to pass. The seven fat cows and lush ears of grain represented seven years of abundance and plenty in Egypt. The seven thin, sickly cows and the seven thin, dried ears of grain represented seven years of famine in the land. The dreams were the same. The bad years would devour all the abundance and plenty of the previous years harvest. The land would not produce enough and the people will lack sufficient food supply. Joseph did not stop there. He went on to recommend a solution to the king. Joseph proposed the king should select and establish a wise man to organize the collection and storage of grain during the years of plenty to be sold and distributed during the years of famine ensuring Egypt would not be devastated by the impending famine.

Pharaoh liked the suggestions and promoted Joseph over all, second only to himself, and it was Joseph's responsibility to see to it that during the years of abundance appropriate supplies would be stored for the lean years to come in Egypt. The king placed on Joseph's hand a ring and gave him wealth and riches. In one day, Joseph went from rags to riches. God's favor was with Joseph and all he did prospered and brought forth good results.

Joseph's Dream Fulfilled (Genesis 45)

All Joseph told Pharaoh came true. The famine reached over all the land, well beyond the borders of Egypt. Jacob, Joseph's father, sent his sons to Egypt to buy food during the famine. When Joseph saw his brothers, he immediately knew them, but they did not recognize him. After two trips to Egypt from their home to buy food, Joseph revealed his identity to them: "I am the brother you sold into slavery. What you meant for my harm, God turned to good." Joseph explained to his brothers that it was God's doing to prepare him for such a time.

Joseph's brothers were afraid that he might want revenge, but Joseph was eager to see the rest of his family. He told his brothers to hurry home and pack up the entire family, his father, and all they owned and to come to a place that had been especially selected and prepared for them. Jacob and his entire family went to Egypt and dwelled in the land of Goshen. God's favor was with Joseph and his family, and all he did prospered.

What does this mean?

'Dwell' is defined by Merriam-Webster on-line, an encyclopedia Britannica Company as to remain for a time or to live as a resident. All of us experience problems from time-to-time. Sometimes the very situations or circumstances that began as a wonderful experience turn tragic or disturbing

> **Dwelling is to remain for a time**

without warning. It is during extreme times of peril and trouble that we need a secret resting or hiding place.

The Land of Goshen was that place for the Israelites. It was a place where God cared and tended to the needs of his people until they were strengthened. God wants to provide a place of restoration and perpetual supply for each of us. We all need a place to dwell when troubles arise. It was a real place for the Israelites, but it is a spiritual place for us today. The land of Goshen is symbolic in that it represents a place of provision when times appear dark and lacking. There are personal conditions to residing in the land of Goshen but these requirements pale in comparison to the benefits. The Land of Goshen is not a final destination but a safety zone leading to the ultimate promise God gives to each of us.

To dwell in the land of Goshen requires personal commitment, perseverance, and patience. We must possess a personal commitment to continue believing, saying, and doing with an attitude of worship, praise, and righteousness, in spite of life's obstacles. In the face of mounting disappointments, discouraging events, and overwhelming debts, dwelling requires a dedication to trust in God. It requires perseverance to stay the course and fight the good fight of faith until the fulfillment of the dream is manifest; and patience to stand and endure when fulfillment of the dream takes unexpected and unforeseen turns.

> **From the pit, through slavery in the house of Potiphar on to prison for the Promise**

Joseph's dreams never revealed that his journey would lead him from a pit (because of his brothers' betrayal) to Potiphar's house (where he was a slave), to prison (as a wrongly accused convict), before his arrival at the king's palace. Joseph's dream only showed the final destination, his family bowing to him. It was up to Joseph to continue to believe for his future in spite of hardships and problems. It is the same for us. While pursuing the promise of our destiny, there will be times when we encounter devastations that seem insurmountable. It is during these times that we on purpose decide to dwell in Goshen.

For God so loved the world,
that he gave his only begotten
Son, that whosoever believeth in
him should not perish, but have
everlasting life.

(John 3:16)

It was a Tuesday, a day that started much like any other day—but it was a day I will never forget. As I hurried to the car to get my daughter to school and then make the forty-five-minute commute to my office, a foreboding sense of doom hung in the early morning air, like an invisible but dense fog. I had an apprehensive and anxious sense that something was wrong, that trouble was around the corner. As I drove toward my office, I tried to pray. I remember asking God to show me why I was having such dark feelings. My son Jonathan crossed my mind, but I was too preoccupied with my ominous thoughts to linger on Jonathan. Boy, did I miss God's signal on this one.

As I drove, the morning darkness gave way to a beautiful, bright, clear blue sky, and the warmth of the sun coming through the windshield of my car provided temporary relief from my ominous feelings. Still, the nagging sensation that something was incredibly wrong lingered. I prayed, "God show me what is happening," and I immediately felt a sense of comfort. Although the sense of dread was still heavy, it was as if I was not alone in the car. Then, I remember being distracted by something—I don't remember what distracted me, but it caused me to lose my train of thought, and I quickly forgot to listen for God's response to my prayer. I remember driving a few more miles, and Jonathan crossed my mind again. I saw his face, and I remembered our conversation from the previous night.

Jonathan and I had had a heated mother-son conversation the night before about his being fiscally responsible in his spending. I was angry with him for having overspent his monthly allowance so early in the month. I was convinced that it was my duty to ensure he handle money matters properly and be fiscally accountable. I reprimanded him for being irresponsible and told him how disappointed I was in him for not using his money wisely. He, of course, apologized, and we said good night, with me reminding him of the great sacrifice and financial burden his being away at school was on the entire family.

The conversation from the previous night crossed my mind and then it was gone. My mind was racing toward all the things that had to be accomplished that day. I still think about the nagging uneasiness that persisted the rest of the day. *It's Tuesday*, I thought as I traveled to the office that morning. *I'm always uneasy on Tuesdays.* I had convinced myself that Tuesday was the worst day of the week. One year earlier, on a Tuesday in September 2001, the 9/11 disasters occurred. Now, I rationalized that my uneasiness had to be the result of the events from a year earlier. Today was September 10, 2002, and I was being sensitive to the past. It was in this frame of mind that I began and ended the day. In my inner core, I knew that my anxiety had nothing to do with the past but with my future. I just could not put my finger on what was bothering me—or why.

As I finished the day and began my commute home, I received a phone call from my husband who was working in another state. He had not expected to return home from his current work assignment for another couple of weeks, but he had some exciting news. His company had been selected for a new business deal in Hawaii, and he would be part of the team leading the assignment. He was calling to see if the children and I would be interested in joining him in Hawaii for a family vacation. It would be our first family vacation in a long time. We had never been to Hawaii, and that would be a real treat for all of us.

Our middle son, Jonathan, was away at college in Atlanta but planned to come home that weekend. Our older son, Joe, and our youngest child, our daughter Brittany, were with me, so we would all discuss the plans over the weekend. I could not have asked for a better end to the day. My husband received his travel plans; he would fly through Atlanta the next morning, pick up extended plans at his office in Houston, and leave for Hawaii at some point the following week. I thought it was great that our entire family would be home that weekend. With my morning gloominess lifted, I continued home, encouraged and excited.

Then, there it was again—the foreboding feeling surfaced through the excitement. It was a feeling that something was really, really wrong. I decided to phone Jonathan and tell him that maybe I'd overreacted the night before. All day I had wanted to talk with him but never got the chance. Now, I wanted to tell him first about the trip to Hawaii. I phoned him on both his home and cell numbers but without success. I left several messages, the last of which, I mentally noted, was at a few minutes past four o'clock in the afternoon. Jonathan was great about returning my calls so I knew I would hear from him soon. I called my older son and told him that Jonathan and his father were coming home that weekend, and we had a big surprise we wanted to discuss. When he pressed me a bit about the surprise, I spilled the beans and told him about his dad's new assignment in Hawaii and our Hawaiian vacation.

I picked up my daughter, Brittany, from school that afternoon and told her the plans. We were all so excited, yet the nagging feeling persisted. No matter how much I tried to calm my inner voice, I knew something was wrong. Brittany and I were on our way to evening service at our church when I remembered that Jonathan had not returned my calls from the afternoon. I asked Brittany to try him again, but he still didn't answer. Now, I connected with the anxiety. Maybe the way I'd felt all day had to do with Jonathan—but then I dismissed the thought. I prayed, felt better, and went to church.

After evening service, I still felt anxious about talking with Jonathan, but I did not yet feel panicked. Bible study was very encouraging, and although I don't remember the specifics, I do know I left feeling reassured of God's love for me. Brittany and I tried calling Jonathan as soon as we got to the car, but again, there was no answer on either of his phones. We called my son Joe and told him we had been trying to reach Jonathan all day. "Have you talked with Jonathan today?" I asked. Joe told us no, but he would call some of their mutual friends in Atlanta and ask if they had talked with or seen Jonathan. Now my mind was racing. It was not like Jonathan to ignore my calls and messages. I told myself, *Don't panic. God loves you. Nothing has gone wrong. If it had, you would know. You would feel it in your core. Mothers know these things; they know when something has gone wrong with their children.* I convinced myself that everything was okay, and I held on to that for the remainder of the evening.

Jonathan never called.

And now, Israel, what doth the LORD thy God require of thee, but to fear the LORD thy God, to walk in all his ways, and to love him, and to serve the LORD thy God with all thy heart and with all thy soul.

(Deuteronomy 10:12)

CHAPTER 1:
The Land of Goshen

Goshen is a special place in Egypt that was prepared especially for Joseph's family to live during Egypt's famine. It was never meant to be a permanent place for the Israelites; rather, it was a place of resource, provision, and refuge during this difficult period. After Joseph was reunited with his family, he instructed his brothers to go home and get all they owned, along with their father, wives, children, and kinsman, and come into the land of Goshen. It was there that their needs would be supplied during the harsh, barren, and trying times to come (Genesis 45).

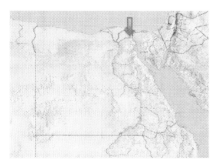

In Genesis 46, God speaks to Jacob (Israel) and makes his provision and plan known—that God will use Joseph to ensure his family's dwelling and provision in the land of Goshen.

God spoke to Israel in a vision that night: "Jacob! Jacob!" "Yes?" he said. "I'm listening." God said, "I am the God of your father. Don't be afraid of going down to Egypt. I'm going to make you a great nation there. I'll go with you down to Egypt; I'll also bring you back here. And when you die, Joseph will be with you; with his own hand he'll close your eyes."
Genesis 46:2-4 (The Message Bible)

In the second year of the famine, the Israelites settled in the land of Ramses in the land of Goshen. Goshen is described as having been the best land in Egypt, suitable for both crops and livestock. In 1885, mathematician E. H. Neville identified Goshen as the twentieth district of Egypt, located in the eastern delta. It covered the western end of the Wadi Tumilat; the eastern end was the district of Succoth, and it extended north as far as the ruins of Pi-Ramesse (known as the "land of Ramses"). Goshen was in Egypt but separate. It was not of Egypt. Joseph had especially selected this land for his family.

Joseph knew times were hard, and they would get tougher throughout the region before getting better, and he wanted his family to be in a place where he could watch and assist them. It was not by accident that God raised Joseph to his position. It was for a time such as this when his people would need help and assistance. God is Lord God Jehovah-jirah—(jirah means He who will provide). He provides for those he loves.

> *Joseph then spoke to his brothers and his father's family. "I'll go and tell Pharaoh, 'My brothers and my father's family, all of whom lived in Canaan, have come to me. The men are shepherds; they've always made their living by raising livestock. And they've brought their flocks and herds with them, along with everything else they own.' When Pharaoh calls you in and asks what kind of work you do, tell him, 'Your servants have always kept livestock for as long as we can remember—we and our parents also.' That way he'll let you stay apart in the area of Goshen—for Egyptians look down on anyone who is a shepherd"*
> Genesis 46:31-34 (The Message Bible).

God's plan for us is for good and not evil. Joseph's dream did not include the pit, Potiphar, or prison, but his dream promised the palace. The hardships Joseph endured—and likewise we endure—are not to destroy us but to bring us to our place of provision and total dependence in God. The land of Goshen symbolizes for each of us our place of provision. It is not our final destination; it is the place we are to bloom where planted for a season. It may not be our Canaan, but it is our port during the storms of life, where God himself sees to our needs. Dwelling in the land of Goshen does not mean that the storm is not raging all around us. It reminds us that no matter the hardship or the struggle, God already has gone before us, his loved ones, and he has made a place of provision. It is truth, even when it does not feel as if it is so. We have to believe it is so, say so, and live so.

Then Joseph came and told Pharaoh, and said, My father
and my brethren, and their flocks, and their herds, and all that they
have, are come out of the land of Canaan; and, behold,
they are in the land of Goshen.

And Pharaoh spake unto Joseph, saying, Thy father
and thy brethren are come unto thee:
The land of Egypt is before thee; in the best of the land make thy
father and brethren to dwell; in the land of Goshen let them dwell:
and if thou knowest any men of activity among them, then make them
rulers over my cattle. And Joseph placed his father and his brethren,
and gave them a possession in the land of Egypt, in the best of the
land, in the land of Rameses,
as Pharaoh had commanded.
Genesis 47:1, 5-6, 11-12 (The Message Bible)

And Israel dwelt in the land of Egypt, in the country of Goshen; and
they had possessions therein, and grew, and multiplied exceedingly.
Genesis 46:27 (Amplified Bible)

And he bowed himself, and said,
What is thy servant, that thou
shouldest look upon such a dead
dog as I am?

(2 Samuel 9:8)

CHAPTER 2:
Lodebar

As the land of Goshen is an example of the extreme measure to which God will go to ensure provision for his children, Lodebar is the culmination of the extreme lack that his children can experience when they are not in his will. In 2 Samuel 9, we see a glimpse into how we, as kings and royal priests, can squander God's extreme measures of provision when we do not understand who—and whose—we are.

The Beginning (2 Samuel 9)

One day, King David reminisced about the good times and his great friendship with Jonathan, son of King Saul, and their exploits in their youth together. He asked his servants, "Is there yet any that is left of the house of Saul, that I may shew [show] him kindness for Jonathan's sake?"

One of King David's servants said, "Yes, there is one who might know." He told King David of Ziba, a servant who had also served King Saul, and that Ziba might know if any of Jonathan's descendants were still living. So King David sent for this servant, Ziba, and asked him, "Is there not yet any of the house of Saul, that I may show the kindness of God unto him?"

And Ziba told the king, "Jonathan has a son. He is a cripple, but he is Jonathan's son." King David asked, "Where is he?" Ziba told the king, "He is in a place called Lodebar." King David sent for Jonathan's son out of Lodebar. Jonathan's son was named Mephibosheth, and he was the grandson of King Saul.

Mephibosheth was brought before King David. He fell on his face and gave reverence to the king. It was then that King David let him know that he had brought him there to show him favor, not to harm him. King David had compassion for Jonathan's son. He told Mephibosheth, "Don't be afraid. I will surely show you kindness for Jonathan, your father's, sake. I will restore all the land of King Saul to you. Your inheritance will be granted to you. And you shall eat at my table, the king's table from this day forth."

Mephibosheth bowed his head after hearing the news and said, "What am I but a dead dog that you should bestow this great honor upon me?" The king, not responding to Mephibosheth's self-portrait, called for and spoke to Ziba and said, "I have given to Jonathan, Mephibosheth's father, all that once belonged to his father, King Saul. It is now the inheritance of Jonathan's son, including you and your fifteen sons and their households and your twenty servants. You, Ziba, and your family shall work the land for Mephibosheth and gather the goods that he may have provision, but he, Mephibosheth, will eat at my table from this day forward." So Mephibosheth lived in Jerusalem and did eat all his meals at the king's table.

Mephibosheth's Challenge

> *For as he thinketh in his heart, so is he.*
> Proverbs 23:7a.

Mephibosheth had a self-image problem. A lot of really bad things had happened to him and his family in his lifetime, beginning in his youth. Mephibosheth was born a prince in the house of King

Saul. His paternal grandfather and father were killed in battle at the Mount of Gilboa, along with Saul's other sons, Abinadi and Melchishua, by the Philistines. As the family was fleeing from their home Mephibosheth's nurse slipped and dropped the child, causing him to be permanently paralyzed. He was taken to a place far from the palace to be hidden away.

I can imagine that Mephibosheth's life must have been a hard one. He was left with no family ties to speak of and no money to sustain him. He was royalty but lived a life devoid of prominence. His circumstances did not reflect his royal bloodline. His body betrayed him in all respects, as he was a cripple. He dwelled in a dismal place and state of mind. It would have been a challenging life, even for a child who was beautiful and healthy. Life was even more uncomfortable for an orphan who was neither beautiful nor whole and certainly not valued.

> **As a man thinks so he is**

Lodebar was not a thriving metropolis but a hiding place off the beaten track. It was a ghetto where hope was almost nonexistent. We hear of children who grow up in extreme poverty or war zones and face daily challenges, just to survive their environments. The traumatic stress of living in such places leaves them emotionally scarred with little self-worth. These are places where food is scarce; housing is below average; and crime, helplessness, and hopelessness are prevalent everywhere and among all age groups. Children learn to be invisible as best they can, so as not to draw the wrath of overworked and overburdened parents and guardians, who have not realized their dreams of full and accomplished lives. Violence is prone to break out at any time, inside and outside of the home. It is a place of isolation and desolation. The grass is not green, and the trees are almost none existent in these places. Nothing beautiful and uplifting abides in Lodebar.

Mephibosheth's Answer

Mephibosheth had no one encouraging him or speaking to him about a bright and wonderful future. There was no person in his ear singing praises about what a wonderful young man he was becoming as he grew into adulthood. He had no one to appreciate his gifts and talents in spite of his handicap. He found himself in an environment where everyone was scratching out an existence, and there was no time for him to be appreciated and reminded of the lineage of kings from whence he was born. Instead, beginning at the age of five, Mephibosheth was told that his birthright had to be hidden forever if he was to live. The people caring for Mephibosheth told him that his grandfather had tried unsuccessfully to kill King David many times. They told Mephibosheth that his aunt Michel had been married to King David and had despised, laughed at, and called King David a fool because he had danced before God. The people caring for Mephibosheth thought they understood King David's motives for seeking relatives of Jonathan. In their minds, the King had sufficient cause to hate Mephibosheth because of his grandfather, King Saul. Mephibosheth had been told his entire life that his identity had to be hidden to protect him from sure destruction. Instead of being educated and instructed as a prince, Mephibosheth believed he had no worth or value because of his gandfather's actions against the king. He believed he was doomed and so he expected the worst and often received the worst of humanity. It was very difficult for him to expect anything other than disappointment, betrayal, and evil.

It was in the midst of this depressing and oppressive life that King David's men found Mephibosheth. He was lacking in everything.

We are the children of the King

Rather than a princely countenance, he had one of total defeat and despair. I can only imagine the dread that filled his heart when the king's men summoned him. He probably assumed that this was the end that he had always thought would find him; death at the hands of the King. His trip to stand before the king must have been one of absolute fear and horror. He could not in his wildest dreams have imagined the wonderful gift that was to be bestowed upon him. Thus, in one day, Mephibosheth went from rags to riches because of his distinguished bloodline. We, too, are the children of a king, yet we live as paupers because we have a self-image problem, the same as Mephibosheth. We look at our circumstances and situations, and we believe them to be our truth. Maybe we live in a place called Lodebar, but the truth is that we are the King's children, and we are only in Lodebar as a result of our choice to remain there. We can make a different choice; we can choose to dwell in the land of Goshen. It is, of course, our choice.

Jesus said unto him, Thou shalt love the Lord thy God with all thy heart, and with all thy soul, and with all thy mind.

(Matthew 22:37)

CHAPTER 3:
Love God

There are many days when my husband and I evaluate our past, and we feel as if we have missed God in so many ways. When I speak of "missing God," I am referring to our responses to situations in our lives. How I feel about my conduct greatly influences my view of myself. When I think that I have disappointed the people I care about the most and who are closest to me, such as my parents, husband, or children, I feel bad and ashamed of who I am and what I may or may not have done. I want them to be proud of me. It is the same when I think about how God sees me. I have this insatiable desire to please God, and I understand that the way in which I treat others is directly tied to my pleasing God, yet on many days, I wonder if I have done the right thing or made the right choices when it comes to how I treat, react, and respond to others. I wonder so many times if I've done the right thing and made the right decisions in God's eyes.

Most days, I know I have not lived up to God's expectation, and I think how love-weary he must be with me. It is on those days, especially, that I remind myself that God loves me, and he loved me first. I say it aloud so I can hear and be reminded of John 3:16—"For God so loved the world that he gave his only begotten Son, that whosoever believeth in him should not perish but have everlasting life." I remind myself that even in my sinful state of mind, God loves me still, and he loves me more than anything else. God withheld not even his own Son for me. God gave his Son as a ransom for me and his Son gave his life. Jesus went to Calvary just for me.

That has to mean something. I struggle so often with the concept of a great big God loving insignificant little me, especially when I think about all my frailties, flaws, and issues. Why me? I can be so unlovable.

Yet all I know for sure is that he loves me. Then why do I continue not to love him back the way I want to and should? I experience every day the challenges that Paul writes about in Romans:

We know that the Law is spiritual; but I am a creature of the flesh [carnal, unspiritual], having been sold into slavery under [the control of] sin.
For I do not understand my own actions [I am baffled, bewildered]. I do not practice or accomplish what I wish, but I do the very thing that I loathe [which my moral instinct condemns].
Now if I do [habitually] what is contrary to my desire, [that means that] I acknowledge and agree that the Law is good (morally excellent) and that I take sides with it.
However, it is no longer I who do the deed, but the sin [principle] which is at home in me and has possession of me.
Romans 7:14-17 (Amplified Bible)

I realize that the first step in my journey toward dwelling in the land of Goshen is to get hold of my mind; if I control my thought-life, I can control my actions and deeds. If I need changes in my life, first I must begin with how I think. Then, I possibly can put to death the deeds of this body.

For if you live according to [the dictates of] the flesh, you will surely die. But if through the power of the [Holy] Spirit you are [habitually] putting to death (making extinct, deadening) the [evil] deeds prompted by the body, you shall [really and genuinely] live forever.
Romans 8:13 (Amplified Bible)

There is nothing we can do to justify or deserve the love of God—nothing. It does not matter how good we are, or how pretty, or how much we practice weight management, or how accomplished we are in our pursuits. God loves us just as we are, and he knows each of us, the real person, and he still loves us. There is nothing we can do to stop his love for us. Therefore, our only practical response to his committed love is to love him back. But the question that constantly comes to mind is, how should we? We all have read the Scripture that says:

And He replied to him, You shall love the Lord your God with all your
heart and with all your soul and with all your mind (intellect).
Matthew 22:37 (Amplified Bible)

I do love God, but how do I show a great big God that I, a little nobody, love him? What do I have to give to such a wonderful God who is eternally committed to loving me? Then I read the Scripture that says,

And now, Israel, what doth the Lord thy God require of thee, but to
fear the Lord thy God, to walk in all his ways, and to love him, and to
serve the Lord thy God with all thy heart and with all thy soul.
Deuteronomy 10:12

I love God with all my heart and soul. If anyone asks me if I love God, my immediate response is a resounding yes—without hesitation. And of course, I would have to be pretty stupid not to fear—in the sense that I have relevant respect for—a God that upholds the world by the word of his power. Yet when I step back to take a good look at the landscape of my life,

> **Love God with all your heart, soul and mind**

when I put my thoughts on hold for a moment—young people call it pausing—and evaluate my responses to life's situations and circumstances, I realize that the fruit borne of my tree does not represent righteousness. My lifestyle does not reflect my professed love for God.

After careful evaluation, I realize that although I believe I love God, I'm having a challenge expressing my true love for God through my actions and deeds. I often have an issue with loving or even liking others. I am challenged when it comes to letting my "little light shine" when things are uncomfortable or when dis-ease creeps into my environment. When I evaluate myself against Deuteronomy 10:12 and Matthew 22:39, I come up short.

> *And the second is like unto it, thou shalt love thy neighbor as thyself*
> Matthew 22:39

In times when I should have compassion for others, I withhold my compassion. There are times when people rub me the wrong way or are unlovable, and I revoke my love and attention immediately. There are times when forgiveness is warranted on both sides of an issue, and I do not readily forgive, even though I know it is the will of God that I forgive and restore others. When I review the film of my Christian walk, I am embarrassed that I call myself a public relations person for Jesus. How must God feel with me as his spokesperson? I remember thinking, *What do non-Christians think about God after an encounter with me?* I ask myself often, "Does my behavior mean I do not love God?" I do love God. I constantly argue the point with myself, attempting to justify and convince myself that my position is okay. Yes, I know there is no condemnation, but I want to do better. I want to improve in the areas that I have not mastered. My life's desire is to hear God say, "Well done, my good and faithful servant." Therefore, I have to work on the areas needing improvement, one by one.

As I begin this journey of self-awareness and improvement, I am constantly challenged to justify my stance on things—I want to make excuses for why I do the things I do. Can I blame my parents? They were demanding and set high expectations, but they were loving and forgiving of my faults. And even if I could, I should not try to lay the blame on them. Can I blame the people with whom I associate? The church I attend? The career I chose? I could insist that those other people led me to act the way I do. If I don't turn the other cheek, is it their fault for creating the unforgiving, insensitive, easily offended monster that I sometimes become? On Sundays, I sometimes act better—but not always. Sometimes on Sundays, in the house of God, if people are not careful, my emotions and feelings get the best of me and cause me to act in a manner uncharacteristic of a Christian. It is hard to do self-examinations and even harder to admit that maybe I am the problem.

As I look deeper, I am ashamed of the hurt I cause our Father when I have not resisted the temptations to react badly to life's situations and circumstances. My flesh craves satisfaction. It is difficult and uncomfortable to discipline my emotions and not get carried away by them. I want to tell people off. I want to

> **Loving God is to obey and serve**

satisfy this fleshly craving to feel better any way necessary, even at the expense of the gospel. These are the emotions I wanted so desperately to satisfy—until I learned there is a better approach to life. Now I am pregnant with the desire to do better.

I realize that to love God is to exercise my ability to make the choice to obey and honor God. It is not out of fear that I want to obey God but out of love. I realize there is a direct correlation between my obeying, honoring, and serving God and the level of satisfaction and achievement I attain in my life. When I say I love God, I am professing that he is my Lord, and I will do everything within my power to obey his voice and commands and honor him. I will simply do what he says to do. It is as simple as that. I've made it so hard for myself for so many years. Now, when I look back, I wonder how I allowed the enemy to control me for so long. Development comes from renewing the mind through revelation, which only comes through hearing the Word of God. Renewing the mind is a new way to see things, a new perspective. I've decided that I am on the Lord's side, so I hate the devil and all he stands for; he is my enemy. The Bible asks what light has to do with darkness. The answer is absolutely nothing. That is the mind-set I have established in my life. In my daily walk, I have to make choices with regard to how I will respond before I arrive at certain decisions. I have to make up my mind intentionally that I am going to treat people well, no matter how they respond to me or treat me. Living purposefully is an imperative, if promotion is desired in this Christian development process. I will have to change—that is the bottom line. Let me share a true story to illustrate.

I believe that everyone who has been abused, mistreated, harshly held accountable, or hated will ask, at some point, "Why me?" He or she will look around at others and work hard to be anyone other than who he truly is. These individuals (including me), while possessing varying gifts, seldom become all they are capable of becoming and rarely arrive at their true destinations of achievement.

Far too many never break the cycle of self-abuse, because their value in their own eyes is diminished. When we devalue ourselves because of how we *think* others see us, we limit God in us. I once worked for a wonderful engineering firm—one of the largest aerospace companies in the world—where I tried to gain the respect of my peers. I wanted so much for others to see me as a good person, a good employee, and a good corporate citizen—the opinions of those around me mattered.

I had been with the firm for a few years when I had a nagging, constant urge regarding our vice president's wife. I had seen her a couple of times at our company's events but did not know anything about her. Still, I had a feeling that she and I had a special bond. I always have known that I have the special gift of healing. When I lay hands on the sick, they do recover. I know there are many people who do not believe in supernatural healing, but there are gifts assigned to some that are undeniable. I have such a gift . . .

and because I believe I have the gift of healing I act on it. I am sure there are special people assigned to do miraculous and special things for others, and I am sure that the vice president's wife was a special assignment of mine. My assignment was to pray for healing for her . . . but I refused, not because I did not want to, but I was afraid to cross social boundaries.

Over the next several years, my nagging concern for her grew. I heard God's voice many times, telling me to pray for her. I refused again and again. *Who am I to pray for her?* I thought. I could imagine the reaction if I walked up to the vice president—the highest ranking person at our facility—and said, "God told me to pray for your wife." I did not know him personally, nor did I know if he and his wife were Christians. The only thing I did know was that I heard God say to pray for this woman. I thought I was crazy—only God knows what they would think. I made a choice to fear what this man would think about me rather than to love God so much that I would obey him, even though I did not understand it.

I never found a convenient time to offer prayer to her. I made myself believe I could not do this, but the reality is that I *would not* do it. I would not obey God in this matter. It is so strange yet so common that we rationalize and reason according to our limited understanding, instead of trusting God. Our obedience should not be reliant upon what we know but on whose we are.

I know when I hear the voice of God. I know that when it absolutely makes no sense. He is the one who is speaking. I struggled with the desire to obey God for more than three years, resisting it. Then, one night at a company-sponsored function, this particular vice president sat at a table with me. This man and I were on such different levels in the company's hierarchy that I kept asking myself, "Why is he sitting at my table, with all the tables in this place from which to choose? He's a former astronaut, one of the top leaders in this company. Why is he sitting with me?"

We talked during dinner and interacted with one another on a level I had not known previously. He was a vice president, and I was a mere engineering manager. The distance between our titles was more of a gulf than a gap. Still, we sat, ate dinner and talked. He told me that his son had been murdered while away at college. He talked about his family's struggles through the days of grief and hurt, and he went on tell me how they had stood together as a family. They had fought to grieve together as one and live on together, while keeping his son's memory alive. He was a very special man who had flown fighter jets in the armed services and commanded the space shuttle on several missions to the international space station. One thing is clear: he understood the principle of command and control. He understood how to obey orders from a higher source, even if he did not understand them, to get a mission accomplished. That night, he modeled a natural behavior of obedience that I marvel at, even today. I know it was God's hand that sent him to sit with me, to show me how to obey.

Two years after that fateful evening, my family experienced an incredible loss, one that struck my family's core. My son Jonathan had a massive heart attack and died while away at college. There had been no warning, no sweet good-byes; there was only a phone call of condolence from an Atlanta police officer. During my months of grief and recovery, I thought many times of that night a national hero had obeyed God and lightened a load for me that I had not known was coming.

I have tried to replay our conversation so many times when grief and sorrow threatened to tear apart my heart, my marriage, and my family. I remember his saying to me that his remaining two children were doing especially well. He and his wife were new grandparents, and their marriage was strong. His exact words are unimportant now, but what he planted in my heart and mind that night is something that I held tight during the months of agony after losing my child. His saying that all was well with him and his family gave me strength to breathe during the early days of our loss.

I thank God that he obeyed God and sat with me that night. I am sure that our conversation that night was not the only factor that saved my mind, but it was a major contribution to my understanding my part in this life's storyboard. I cannot imagine the grief of a family who loses a child in such a violent and destructive way as they did. If they could survive, then so could I. I would live one day at a time—for my husband, my parents, my living children, and my extended family.

That vice president obeyed God that night, years before my tragedy, but I had not done so with regard to his wife. I thought to do so would hurt my career, my chances for advancement. I would not obey God because I thought perhaps people would think me a religious fanatic or nut case. I did not see myself in the right perspective. I did not consider that I was an instrument of God. I basically told God to use someone else for this task. I was too concerned with how others would see me. God wanted to use my hands for good, but I would not surrender them to him. Yet someone did for me what I was unwilling to do for another.

I felt awful after realizing how I had failed. During my time of recovery, I began to pray for this vice president's family and especially his wife. I was later told she had battled cancer, and it was in remission. The joy I felt upon hearing this was healing salve to an open wound of regret and remorse. I was so happy that they had won another great victory. It was after I returned to work and during another company-sponsored social event that I had an opportunity to see them. I wanted to let her know how her husband had encouraged me to live after my son's death through his conversation many years before. I wanted to say how hard it must have been for her husband to share those very painful memories with me. I wanted to say to her how much I admired her strength and courage in keeping her family—and especially her children—focused on their destiny. I wanted to say that her family's struggles had motivated me to live for my family . . . but I couldn't. I didn't. I simply hugged her and walked away. I am sure she still wonders about the strange employee who hugged her so tightly that night.

Afterward, I realized that loving God meant to obey him, even if I did not understand. We do not know how our roles intersect and assist other lives; only God knows. When God prompts us to do good, even if it seems crazy, it is for a purpose.

God makes a way of escape for us. We can walk circumspectly before men. We can love God with all our heart and soul by making choices and decisions to be an imitator of Christ, before, during, and after the challenge. I choose to love God. Loving God causes me to obey, serve, and honor him. Loving God causes me to set my will to obey his commands and serve him through my lifestyle. Loving God causes me to dwell in the land of Goshen, because I no longer am a slave to my circumstances, situations, issues, trials, or tests. I am an "overcomer," and my joy is established and set. He sees to my prosperity and success, because I trust in him, even when I do not understand it all.

Step 1: Love God

Jesus said unto him, Thou shalt love the Lord thy God with all thy heart, and with all thy soul, and with all thy mind.
This is the first and great commandment.
Matthew 22:37-38

Final Thought:

Simply, love God. When we make the commitment to love God, we make him Lord. We are no longer in control, nor do we get to make independent decisions and choices. Loving God is the first step to dwelling in the land of Goshen.

Because they rebelled against the words of God, and contemned the counsel of the most High: [12]Therefore he brought down their heart with labor; they fell down, and there was none to help.

(Psalm 107:11-12)

Chapter 4:
Seek Wisdom

One evening I was invited to a special gathering at my sister-in-law's home. I had no idea what to expect, but I entered the house with anticipation. There seemed to be something special in the air—it was as if I knew something good was about to happen, especially for me. After some small talk and a few refreshments, my sister-in-law introduced her special guest, who began to explain why we had been invited there that evening—she wanted to tell us about a wonderful career opportunity. She was a Mary Kay Cosmetics sales director, and my sister-in-law had joined the organization and was looking to share this business with us.

My heart sank. *Oh no*, I thought. *I don't want to sell cosmetics.* I was hoping for something better, something different—and anything other than cosmetics. My excitement about the evening drained from me. I could feel the heat in my cheeks and the agitation rising in my countenance. I no longer wanted to be in this place. I wanted to bolt toward the door but felt a flash of shame at such inappropriate behavior. *I cannot act that way in front of my in-laws*, I reasoned. *I'll just sit here politely until she finishes her pitch, and then I'll decline as nicely as possible. Surely even this sales director will understand and appreciate that I am an engineer and far too qualified to sell cosmetics door-to-door.* During the presentation, however, I found myself somewhat interested. The sales director showed us some of her previous checks. "Full disclosure," she told us. She made more money as a Mary Kay sales director than she ever had made as a CPA. She was well spoken and gracious in every way, I realized, and I discovered during her presentation that she and I had much in common. She had completed college. She was passionate and accomplished in her career. She even shared that when she first was asked to join Mary Kay Cosmetics, her sentiments were the same as mine—and she rejected the offer. She eventually joined for the tax benefits and the opportunity to run her own business.

"Tax benefits? What tax benefits?" I asked. She shared the concept of the business. As an independent cosmetic consultant, working with Mary Kay Cosmetics, we were business owners and would be able to receive the same tax benefits as other small businesses. She explained that each consultant is trained in all aspects of the business, and the rewards are commensurate with how much effort and time the business owner is willing to dedicate to "minding her business." After she answered a few additional questions from the guests, more than a few of us decided to join. It was probably one of the best decisions I have ever made.

What a turn-about that night. I signed with Mary Kay Cosmetics and never looked back. During my tenure with the company, I earned the use of two red Pontiac Grand Ams, one pink Grand Prix, and two pink Cadillacs. How did I do it? I had to change my way of thinking. My pastor calls it "emptying the cup." Let me explain. It is impossible to fill a cup that already is full. If a cup is full, it first must be emptied of what is occupying the space before a new substance can be added.

Do not be conformed to this world (this age), [fashioned after and adapted to its external, superficial customs], but be transformed (changed) by the [entire] renewal of your mind [by its new ideals and its new attitude], so that you may prove [for yourselves] what is the

good and acceptable and perfect will of God, even the thing which is
good and acceptable and perfect [in His sight for you].
Romans 12:2 (Amplified Bible)

This was the beginning of my exercising my ability to seek out and venture past the status quo. I had to take a chance on something I did not fully understand and trust there were knowledgeable others to teach me. It was not a get-rich-quick scheme; rather, it was a step-by-step process and disciplined program to assist me in achieving my dreams. It required much effort, belief, and sacrifice, but little by little—learning, doing, and becoming each day—I excelled.

I had no idea of the wealth of knowledge and wisdom with which I would come into contact as I learned the business. I have to admit I did not have high expectations at first—I didn't want to set myself up to be disappointed when it all fell apart. Still, I became a student of the business, eager to learn all I could to be successful. This is where my real education in life began. During the early months, the training focused on the fundamentals of running a successful business, with emphasis on the cosmetic products and services we provided. The training focused on knowing the products, demonstration, and closing-the-sale mechanics to achieve sales projections, establishing and attaining recruitment goals, and basic business acumen.

After a short period with the company, I achieved the status of sales director. I attended my first director's training in Dallas, Texas, and was able to spend quality time with key leadership and the founder of the company, Mary Kay Ash. During the week-long training, Mary Kay taught us life lessons I will never forget. She was a petite woman, but her heart and love for people filled the room. She had a presence about her I could not articulate then, but now I understand—she had an anointing (anointing is a passion). She greeted the new directors, and we settled in, expecting to hear her encourage us to meet our business projections and tell us about the basics of the company. Her talk that day was nothing of the sort. She began by welcoming us and telling us how proud she was of our success and accomplishments. I scanned the room. I wanted to see if others in the room were as affected by her as I was. They were. She was one of the most genuine people I have ever met. Let me share with you what she told us that day as new directors in her company.

Mary Kay Ash told us about loving people. Her talk that day did not concentrate on achieving business projections; it was more like a grandmother telling us to always be aware of the golden rule. She talked about why she started her business. She shared some of her struggles during her marriages, parenting, living and working during an era dominated with male-dominated principles, losing a child to cancer, and building a successful business when no one believed in her. Her mission and ministry were to give other women a chance for independence and self-reliance. She was a visionary who loved and embraced her destiny. Mary Kay Ash is one of my heroes.

After her talk, I asked her if I could speak with her privately; she agreed. I asked her how she knew this would be her life's work. Her answer was that she did not know. Each step of her journey brought her to a new role in life. It was a journey of self-discovery that took a lifetime to really understand. She said it was only through hindsight that she fully saw how God had used her, that if he had shared the entire plan with her from the beginning, she would have thought it impossible—it would have seemed too daunting a task, and she would have given up before she started. She never could have conceived of being used in this way.

That day, she also shared nuggets of wisdom. She told a story about

> **Walk not in the counsel of the ungodly**

running late for church services one Sunday—her only opportunity to attend worship services that week, due to her busy schedule. She was determined to attend a service that Sunday before leaving the city for a week of meetings on the road. She was driving and trying to decide which other church could she attend that morning that was close by. As she was turning a corner, she noticed a building just across the street and realized it was a church. It was small and in need of repairs and painting, but people were arriving for services, so she decided to stop. She entered to find they were preparing to start Sunday school service. Everyone met in the sanctuary for the opening and then would disperse to different parts of the building to study the lesson.

The superintendent of the Sunday school opened the service in what must have been their usual custom and then, when it was time for classes, he announced that the young children's teacher was ill, so the three- to six-year-olds did not have a teacher. He asked for a volunteer to teach this young class. No one responded. After a few minutes, the superintendent said he would take the class. Mary Kay said that she felt the urging of the Holy Spirit to volunteer as the young children's teacher. Though she had never been to this church, she felt as if this was something she was supposed to do. From that day forward—every Sunday, for two years—she taught the children's class at that small Baptist church. She likes to think she made a real difference by volunteering to teach that class. Moments like those, she told us, give her life true meaning and purpose. "Making a difference for others is my greatest pleasure," she said.

She finished her story by saying, "Whatever you spoon into the lives of others always will come back into your life by the shovelful." The Bible says it this way:

Knowing that whatsoever good thing any man doeth, the same shall he
receive of the Lord, whether he be bound or free.
Ephesians 6:8

Mary Kay—a woman who has money, diamonds, furs, large homes, yachts, a loving family, loyal employees, peace, and prosperity—said she feels the happiest and most fulfilled by impacting the lives of others in a positive way; it's what she was placed here to do. She then encouraged each of us to find our "purpose" and to go after it with all our might. I was impressed that for all her wealth, Mary Kay found fulfillment in teaching a Sunday school class. I decided that I wanted to be just like this special woman.

Step 2: Seek Wisdom

BLESSED (HAPPY, fortunate, prosperous, and enviable) is the man
who walks and lives not in the counsel of the ungodly [following their
advice, their plans and purposes], nor stands [submissive and inactive]
in the path where sinners walk, nor sits down [to relax and rest] where
the scornful [and the mockers] gather.
But his delight and desire are in the law of the Lord, and on His law
(the precepts, the instructions, the teachings of God) he habitually
meditates (ponders and studies) by day and by night.
Psalm 1:1-2 (Amplified Bible)

Final Thought:

Proverbs tells us to desire wisdom. Wisdom shared through sound counsel gives us the necessary recipe to make right choices, to reject and dispel myths and untruths, and to motivate us to action. We must pursue wisdom, knowledge, and understanding, and these can be found in expected and unexpected places. Keep your ear and heart open and be ready to hear the tapping of wisdom at your heart and inner core. You will recognize her voice when she speaks. Seeking wisdom and godly counsel is the second step to dwelling in the land of Goshen.

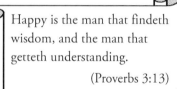

Happy is the man that findeth wisdom, and the man that getteth understanding.

(Proverbs 3:13)

Our son Jonathan never called again—at least not via AT&T. I decided to call him one last time before I went to bed. *Maybe he's returned to his apartment and will be available*, I thought. Although it was well past 10 p.m., I called again. Again, he didn't answer, but this time I had a sense of peace. I remember thinking how strange the sensation felt—it wasn't spooky or frightening, just a sense of well-being. I knew then that everything would be all right. I went to bed, and sleep came immediately. It was a relief as I felt the familiar darkness overtake me. *Tomorrow will be a great day. We have a lot to look forward to,* I remember thinking before I drifted off. *We are all going on a family vacation to Hawaii.*

"Hello." I heard my tired and anxious voice speak into the phone. *When did I answer the phone?* I thought. I glanced at the clock on the nightstand next to the bed. It was after midnight! I thought, *Something bad must have happened for someone to call so late.* In that second, my mind clicked into action. *No, it must be Jonathan returning my call. I am really going to get this young man for not calling me back sooner.* "Hello," I said a second time, expecting to hear my son's voice.

"Hi, Mrs. Kelley? This is Pricilla." I could hear the concern in Jonathan's girlfriend's voice. "I'm calling because I can't reach Jonathan, and I am starting to get very worried."

Okay, I thought. *I am not going to panic or overreact.* I tried to clear my head. "Pricilla? Pricilla, I'm sure everything is all right," I heard myself lie. "He's probably just not made it home yet to check his messages. I am sure everything is okay. I believe I would feel it if something was wrong."

Pricilla responded immediately. "No, ma'am, it's more than that, Mrs. Kelley. I have the pass code to Jonathan's cell phone, and I've been checking his messages all afternoon and evening. He has not picked up his messages since before 2 p.m. today, and that is not like

Jonathan. He checks his messages every fifteen to thirty minutes. Mrs. Kelley, something is wrong."

I was wide awake now. I knew she was right. Jonathan was in college, but he also worked part-time as an entertainment promoter. We teased him that he did not have a "real" job, but he worked hard at his business and seemed very successful at it—he loved working as an entertainment promoter. He kept his phone close to him, and it was on him at all times. Jonathan always returns my calls, no matter where he might be. I had to admit now that his not returning my calls and not picking up his messages were not normal for Jonathan. I told Priscilla I would make some phone calls and get back with her in a few minutes. I immediately called my son Joe, asking if he'd heard from his brother.

"No, I haven't," he answered.

I told him about my conversation with Pricilla, and he said that he too had left messages but had not heard back from Jonathan or his friends in Atlanta. He offered to try again, and I said I'd call my brother, Grady.

Grady McCardell is my younger brother and a police sergeant with the Houston Police Department—I thought he'd know what to do. He said I should call the Atlanta Police Department and ask them to perform a welfare check at his address. I did. I spoke with an Atlanta officer who assured me they would do just that. Then Joe called me back to let me know he spoke with three of Jonathan's friends in Atlanta, and they were on their way to his apartment to check on him. They all told Joe the same story—they had seen Jonathan earlier at school but not since before 2 p.m. I felt a little relieved, knowing his friends were on their way to his address.

After they arrived, they called to let me know his car was parked in his usual spot, so he must be there, but no lights were on in his apartment. They could not remember a time when they had been to his apartment at night and there had been no lights on.

I felt very uneasy now. I knew that Jonathan was afraid of the dark. He would never be in a totally dark apartment. Even if he had fallen asleep earlier in the day, somehow the darkness would have woken him, and he would have gotten up to turn on a light. They said they had called campus security, the apartment security, and the Atlanta police, asking them to check on their friend. While we were talking, they came up with an idea. They remembered that Jonathan always left his balcony sliding glass door unlocked. Jonathan's three friends decided to climb up to Jonathan's third-floor balcony to see if the glass door was unlocked. We hung up, and I held my breath. I prayed. I prayed that no one else's child would get hurt and that my child would be found sound asleep and unhurt in his apartment. Boy, did I pray in those minutes that seemed like forever.

When I could wait no longer, I called Jill, one of the three friends, to see if she could get into the apartment.

I did not hear the phone ring; instead, I heard the most blood-curdling screams imaginable. She must have instinctively answered when her phone rang, but she was screaming, louder than I'd ever heard before. "Mrs. Kelley, Mrs. Kelley, he's blue!" she cried. "Mrs. Kelley, he's cold! Mrs. Kelley! Mrs. Kelley, he's dead!"

My heart stopped. My mind would not work fast enough. I remember hearing myself say, "Please help my son. He is not dead, and he is depending on you. Hang up, and call 911 immediately. Please help my son. He needs you."

I was later told that while we were on the phone, Atlanta police officers were knocking at the door. When I called back minutes later to see if she had reached the emergency personnel, an officer answered the phone. I identified myself as Jonathan's mother, and he immediately said, "I want to give you my condolences."

I immediately corrected him. I said to him, as calmly as I could, "Your condolences are not necessary. My son is not dead."

He repeated his words in a very calm and emotionally sensitive way, assuring me that he had been a police officer for some time, and the young man they had just found was dead. "He appears to have been deceased for some time." He went on to describe the scene. "There are no signs of a struggle. Nothing is out of place or disturbed. The apartment is clean and orderly and looks like a college student lives here." Then he said, "The door was locked from the inside. It appears that your son simply died peacefully in his sleep." Yes, that was the word he used. "Peacefully." I thanked him, pressed the dial button, and called my mother.

Jonathan DeWitt Andrew Kelley

May 9, 1980-September 10, 2002

Therefore I esteem all thy
precepts concerning all
things to be right; and I hate
every false way.

(Psalm 119:128)

CHAPTER 5:
Live Virtuously

Today, I witnessed an amazing act of kindness. While shopping, I noticed a middle-aged woman and a young man, perhaps in his teens, walk up to a young shopper as she was leaving a store. They whispered something to her, but she shook her head as she searched through the fashionable handbag hanging from her shoulder. They seemed to be strangers to her, and she tightened her grip on her handbag, as if to assure herself it was still on her shoulder. It was obvious by the couple's body language and the meek and embarrassed look in their eyes that they were ashamed. I stood watching the threesome, openly intrigued by their interaction. Although it wasn't my intention, I could overhear their conversation.

The young shopper talked with the woman and young man for a few moments and then began to rummage through her purse again, pulling out her wallet. She searched its contents and then looked up from the wallet and gently shook her head. The couple began to walk away with their shoulders drooping, as if all hope was lost. The young shopper watched as the two walked away, and then, after a second or two, she called to them to come back. I overheard her ask them to wait. The young woman walked quickly to the nearest ATM and extracted what looked like a twenty-dollar bill. She approached the couple and handed them the money. Their eyes lit up, and the relief in their eyes could not be missed or understated. They thanked the shopper politely, and then I heard them ask for her address so they could return the money. She declined and smiled at them as she walked toward the parking lot. She appeared happier, lighter, and changed.

Fascinated, I felt lighter and relieved. I noticed that I had a renewed energy, and I walked with a rejuvenated pep in my step. It occurred to me a couple hours later that I was humming. There was a song in my heart, and I had been humming it since I'd seen the encounter at the store. So many times, people who appear to be in need are not what they seem. The scams that people perpetrate upon others are countless and because of this, many people who are usually generous do not offer help, for fear of being tricked by con artists. I, however, had witnessed a random act of kindness, and it made me feel good.

The rest of the story: I watched the couple as they walked away from the young woman shopper. They walked across the store's parking lot to a car at the far end. The young man pulled a gas can from the trunk of an old and battered blue car. The vehicle had a severely cracked front windshield, and it clearly had seen better days. The tires were well worn, and the

> **Give and it shall be given to you**

driver's side door appeared to be jammed, as they struggled to open the door to retrieve something from the front seat. They crossed a major highway underpass on foot to a gasoline station. It seems they had been dependent upon the kindness of a total stranger to pay for gas for their car.

I do not know if that young woman had given the twenty dollars out of her lack or out of her abundance, but I do know that her kindness made the difference in that moment for three total strangers. Two strangers experienced a direct result of her kindness. I, on the other hand, experienced an indirect result. Her kindness inspired me in a way that I had not been touched in a great many years. Her kindness created a compassion capacity in me.

One of my favorite movies is *As Good as It Gets*, starring Jack Nicholson and Helen Hunt. Jack plays a cantankerous man suffering from obsessive-compulsive disorder (OCD) and paranoia. He is afraid or superstitious of everyone and everything and is not a pleasant person to be around. Helen Hunt plays a young woman struggling to make ends meet while working to support herself and to keep a positive attitude. It is her positive attitude toward life, in spite of her seemingly less-than-abundant lifestyle, that attracts Jack to her.

In one scene, Jack's character escorts Helen's character out to dinner at an exclusive restaurant, but Jack is dressed casually. The maître d' tells Jack that he will not be allowed to enter without the appropriate attire—a dinner jacket is required. The maître d' retrieves a dinner jacket for Jack to wear and tries to help him put the jacket on. Jack is appalled—as someone with OCD, he would never wear an item that someone else had worn. Jack leaves the restaurant to buy a new dinner jacket, as Helen waits for him to join her. When Jack arrives back from his shopping expedition in a new dinner jacket, he takes out his frustration on Helen, questioning why he was stopped for not wearing a dinner jacket when she was allowed in the restaurant in a housedress.

Helen had tried to look her best and was insulted by his comment. She stands to leave, but a mortified Jack begs her to stay—not because he wants her company, but because he cannot bear the embarrassment of someone walking out on him. She tells him the only way she will stay is if he says something nice to her. He hesitates, realizes she is serious, and thinks for a moment before saying sincerely to Helen, "Being with you makes me want to be a better man." The impact and effect of those kind words meant the world to her, and she stays only to have Jack say something equally stupid a few minutes later that causes her to leave the restaurant abruptly.

"You make me want to be better." I have never forgotten that scene because of that one line and its tremendous effect on me. I want so much to please God, yet I find it is not that simple for me. I've asked myself what inspires me to be better. People, random acts of kindness, joy, family—there are so many things—but the single most important thing that makes me desire to be better is the Word of God. When I see the Word of God in action, I want to be like that, do those things, and act that way. I want to choose to do the right things. The Word of God makes me want to do and be better.

That nature (creation) itself will be set free from its bondage to decay and corruption [and gain an entrance] into the glorious freedom of God's children.
We know that the whole creation [of irrational creatures] has been moaning together in the pains of labor until now.
And not only the creation, but we ourselves too, who have and enjoy the first fruits of the [Holy] Spirit [a foretaste of the blissful things to come] groan inwardly as we wait for the redemption of our bodies [from sensuality and the grave, which will reveal] our adoption (our manifestation as God's sons).
Romans 8:21-23 (The Amplified Bible)

That's why I don't think there's any comparison between the present hard times and the coming good times. The created world itself can hardly wait for what's coming next. Everything in creation is being more or less held back. God reins it in until both creation and all the creatures are ready and can be released at the same moment into the glorious times ahead. Meanwhile, the joyful anticipation deepens. All around us we observe a pregnant creation. The difficult times of pain throughout the world are simply birth pangs. But it's not only around us; it's within us. The Spirit of God is arousing us within. We're also feeling the birth pangs. These sterile and barren bodies of ours are yearning for full deliverance. That is why waiting does not diminish us, any more than waiting diminishes a pregnant mother. We are enlarged in the waiting. We, of course, don't see what is

enlarging us. But the longer we wait, the larger we become, and the more joyful our expectancy.
Romans 8:18-23 (The Message Bible)

Many are the temptations of our flesh. Even when we seek to do good, evil is present. I want to make right choices, but the wrong choices are seemingly so much more practical. Why is that? We are all spirits that live in a body that possess a soul. In the body (flesh), there dwells no good thing according to scripture. Simply stated, there are times I want to do what I want to do when I want to do it regardless of what the bible says. I want to have my way no matter how much it hurts others or what they think. I want to satisfy my every craving and desire for pleasure. It is not the body but the Spirit that lives inside that desires sincere fellowship and relationship with God. Therefore, a war is raging within. This constant battle for dominance and control between my spirit (the real me) and my human body (the house my spirit dwells in) is ongoing. It is the soul (personality, willful self, will) that must be aligned to the spirit to keep the body under subjection.

But I keep under my body, and bring it into subjection:
lest that by any means, when I have preached to others,
I myself should be a castaway
1 Corinthians 9:27

It is our responsibility to set our mind and heart to obey the laws, commands, and statutes of God. We are living by grace. We all seem to understand grace, but that does not give us a license to live without restraint or regard for others. We each have the choice to live a life of virtue. There is no middle ground. Either we honor God with our right choices, or we dishonor God with our wrong choices. To live a virtuous life is merely to make a decision to do what is right, according to the Word of God. There is no other true measurement of right living than the Word of God. The Word of God is not here to place unfair and burdensome rules upon us; it is an instrument to help gauge and determine rightness without the pollution of emotions and superficial self-gratifying and indulgent doctrines. It already has been established that God loves us. No matter what we do, evil or good, it is all as filthy rags in the sight of God, yet he continues to love us. It is because of God's immense love for us that we should desire to love him back. It is our love for God that compels us to obey and do the right things.

I can remember a time during my youth when a popular slogan was "If it feels good, do it." Many of my generation became involved in premarital sex, drugs, and living "on the edge," rebelling against anything that the previous generations made us feel was wrong. We worked hard to define our own sense of rightness, disregarding anything that anyone else upheld as right. Without an unchanging playbook (the Bible), over time we might have tried to rewrite the definition of righteousness. I searched the Scripture, as I needed to understand what God meant when he stated, "I set before you life and death, blessings and curses, choose ye life."

> **Whatever good any one does the same shall he receive from the Lord**

The Bible is full of rules—thou shalt nots—beginning with the Ten Commandments.

Thou shalt have no other gods before me.
Thou shalt not make unto thee any graven image, or any likeness of any thing that is in heaven above, or that is in the earth beneath, or that is in the water under the earth.
Thou shalt not bow down thyself to them, nor serve them: for I the Lord thy God am a jealous God, visiting the iniquity of the

fathers upon the children unto the third and fourth generation
of them that hate me;
And shewing mercy unto thousands of them that love me,
and keep my commandments.
Thou shalt not take the name of the Lord thy God in vain;
for the Lord will not hold him guiltless that taketh
his name in vain.
Remember the Sabbath day, to keep it holy.
Six days shalt thou labor, and do all thy work:
But the seventh day is the Sabbath of the Lord thy God:
in it thou shalt not do any work, thou, nor thy son, nor thy daughter,
thy manservant, nor thy maidservant, nor thy cattle,
nor thy stranger that is within thy gates:
For in six days the Lord made heaven and earth, the sea, and all that
in them is, and rested the seventh day: wherefore the Lord blessed the
Sabbath day, and hallowed it.
Honor thy father and thy mother: that thy days may be long upon the
land which the Lord thy God giveth thee.
Thou shalt not kill.
Thou shalt not commit adultery.
Thou shalt not steal.
Thou shalt not bear false witness against thy neighbor.
Thou shalt not covet thy neighbor's house, thou shalt not covet thy
neighbor's wife, nor his manservant, nor his maidservant, nor his ox,
nor his ass, nor any thing that is thy neighbor's.
Exodus 20:3-17

Galatians provides a clear description of the works of the flesh—things
we should not be doing as children of the light.

Now the works of the flesh are manifest, which are these; Adultery,
fornication, uncleanness, lasciviousness,
Idolatry, witchcraft, hatred, variance, emulations, wrath, strife,
seditions, heresies, envyings, murders, drunkenness, revelings, and such
like: of the which I tell you before, as I have also told you in time past,

> *that they which do such things shall not*
> *inherit the kingdom of God.*
> Galatians 5:19-21

Abstaining from these things alone does not represent living a life of virtue. Yes, it is true we should obey God, but to live virtuously is so much more than simply not disobeying or not offending God by bending or breaking his laws. Living a virtuous life involves our motives by which we obey the rules and commands and observe the statutes of God. A virtuous life does not mean that you will not sin or offend occasionally. It means that you are working to get to the heart of the matter of why you do what you do. Yes, it is all about the heart.

> *Keep thy* heart *with all diligence; for out of it are the issues of life.*
> Proverbs 4:23

According to my pastor, Andre Carrington, living virtuously is not an automatic product of the new birth. When I receive Jesus as Lord and Savior, I do not automatically want to or know how to live righteously. It is a process as I am exposed to the Word of God, so that this body of sin that I live in can be destroyed.

> *Knowing this, that our old man is crucified with him, that the body of*
> *sin might be destroyed, that henceforth we should not serve sin.*
> Romans 6:6

When I am exposed to the Word of God on a consistent basis and set my mind (or will) to do what is right, my choices align with the Word of God, and I cannot help but live a virtuous life that will please God. One thing is for sure: I cannot make right choices without a steady diet of the Word. It is not enough to simply decide to obey the Ten Commandments, to treat people right, to not fornicate, or to stop living a riotous lifestyle. I have to know and apply the Word of God to my choices and decisions.

Sanctify them through thy truth: thy word is truth.
John 17:17

In the beginning, the evaluation of my choices based on the Word of God must be purposefully and conscientiously made. Then less conscious is this evaluation of choices as we are exposed more and more to the Word of God. As the Word matriculates through every aspect of life, our way of thinking and living is changed. The promises of God are true. When we live a virtuous life of love and obedience, we please God.

When a man's ways please the Lord, he maketh even his
enemies to be at peace with him.
Proverbs 16:7

It is not an overnight accomplishment. As the heart's cleansing agent, the Word of God transforms our thinking; the decisions and choices we make are different. The result is an expectancy of God's favor to show up in every circumstance and situation. We realize that we do not earn anything from God, but as with a good child and his earthly father, our heavenly Father is moved by our obedience and provides. It is not because he has to do so but because our Father wants to give us more than all we can think or ask him to give. He wants to help us prosper more than we want prosperity.

Knowing Beloved, I wish above all things that thou mayest prosper
and be in health, even as thy soul prospereth.
3 John 1:2

Step 3: Live Virtuously

Finally, brethren, whatsoever things are true, whatsoever things
are honest, whatsoever things are just, whatsoever things are pure,
whatsoever things are lovely, whatsoever things are of good report; if
there be any virtue, and if there be any praise, think on these things.
Philippians 4:8

Final Thought:

Philippians helps us understand that it is only through the renewing of our mind and actively seeking to be, do, and live a better life are we protected from the distress and endless suffering that the body of sin produces. When we make right choices and decisions, it leads to our doing good and ultimately producing the fruit of the Spirit (love, joy, peace, long-suffering, gentleness, goodness, and faith). Living a life of virtue can only be achieved on purpose, not by happenstance. Purposely living a virtuous life is the third step to dwelling in the land of Goshen.

And he said unto me, My grace is sufficient for thee: for my strength is made perfect in weakness. Most gladly therefore will I rather glory in my infirmities, that the power of Christ may rest upon me.

(2 Corinthians 12:9)

My husband and I and other family members arrived in Atlanta, Georgia, on September 11, 2002, to identify our son Jonathan DeWitt Andrew Kelley. We held his home-going celebration the following Monday. Even now, it is so surreal. I don't remember much of the festivities. Yes, I refer to them as festivities. It was the last earthly celebration I would ever host for my son. It was a true celebration of life. I felt so privileged to be his mother while he was on earth.

I remember Jonathan's birth as if it were yesterday. He was born on the Friday before Mother's Day, May 9, 1980. Many people warned me that second babies come fast, but I took no heed. When the pains first started, I figured I had time. I was in labor with my first child for close to twelve hours, and I thought there was no need to rush to the hospital. I was wrong. By the time we got to the hospital, Jonathan already was coming through the birth canal. I remember being wheeled into the delivery room, and the doctor desperately rushing to get prepped. He told me to stop pushing, but I told him, "I am not pushing. The child inside me is pushing." When I think back on that day, I smile. As Jonathan burst into this world, I heard a plop, and then the doctor said, "It's a boy." I could see relief on the doctor's face—Jonathan had come out so fast that my doctor actually caught Jonathan in midair. I remember thinking, even back then, that Jonathan sure was in a hurry. I believe Jonathan knew he had a lot of living to do in a very short span of time. Then and now, I consider it a privilege to be his mother.

Jonathan was one of those kids who made everyone smile. He had a heart for people and taught me as much in death as he did in life. He taught me to see people and love them, regardless of their shortcomings and failures. Jonathan had a severe speech impediment, but he never let it stop him. As he grew older, it seemed that when he talked with me, he would stutter more. I remember asking him if I made him nervous. He smiled and answered yes. I smiled at him and asked why. He said, "Mom, you set the bar so high. I worry that I do not live up to your expectations." That was one of the conversations I probably cherish the most. It gave me an opportunity to tell Jonathan how proud of him I truly was. I told him that when I looked at him, I saw a gentle, kind, caring, and accomplished six-foot-two-inch man. I told him that he far surpassed my expectations every day. He grinned, and it was that smile on that day at that moment that I remember when I think of Jonathan. I personally understand what Isaiah was talking about when he wrote Isaiah 6:

In the year that king Uzziah died I saw also the Lord sitting upon a throne, high and lifted up, and his train filled the temple.
Above it stood the seraphims: each one had six wings; with twain he covered his face, and with twain he covered his feet,
and with twain he did fly.
And one cried unto another, and said, Holy, holy, holy, is the Lord of hosts: the whole earth is full of his glory.
And the posts of the door moved at the voice of him that cried, and the house was filled with smoke.
Then said I, **Woe is me! for I am undone**; *because I am a man of unclean lips, and I dwell in the midst of a people of unclean lips: for mine eyes have seen the King, the Lord of hosts.*
Then flew one of the seraphims unto me, having a live coal in his hand, which he had taken with the tongs from off the altar:
And he laid it upon my mouth, and said, Lo, this hath touched thy lips; and thine iniquity is taken away, and thy sin purged.
Also I heard the voice of the Lord, saying, Whom shall I send, and who will go for us? Then said I, Here am I; send me.
Isaiah 6: 1-8

I am so grateful to have had an opportunity to tell Jonathan how proud of him I was. Who would have known that at the end of that very summer, we would be saying good-bye until we meet in eternity.

For many months after Jonathan's death, I thought I could sense or feel his presence with me. At Jonathan's memorial service, I remember Pastor Andre Carrington said I could have confidence that "to be absent from the body is to be present  with God." There have been a number of times since Jonathan departed his physical body when I have heard the front door open and a voice yell, "Lucy, I'm home!" It was Jonathan's special way of greeting me when he returned home after the twelve-hour journey from his school in Atlanta to Houston or from a road trip with friends. It is such a comfort, knowing that we will see each other again.

The funeral director to whom we entrusted the handling of Jonathan's services told our family that Jonathan's funeral was second in size only to one other for which they officiated in their many years of being in business. Parents sent children from Atlanta to be with our family, and Jonathan's boss flew his entire staff to Houston to be with us for his home-going. The family, friends, and coworkers and others that were with us during those trying hours, days, and weeks were many. We were surrounded in love. We needed and appreciated them all. Death really had not been something I had thought much about—not until it was someone dear to me. I lived life as if time was of no consequence. *There always will be tomorrow, and the day after that, and the day after that*, I thought. I still have my moments when the sadness overwhelms me, and I find myself under a cloud of grief and mourning.

My family and I dwell in the Land of Goshen where God provides for us still. It is in the land of Goshen hidden, protected and provided for by God that I heal and seek God's face in this matter. As I struggle with the reality of a child dying while others recover from near-fatal heart attacks and live to testify about it. I am challenged to not succumb to bitterness and jealousy. I am challenged to not feel sorry for my family. I remind myself of the word God spoke into my spirit the first morning we heard the news. God said, "My grace is sufficient." God's grace is sufficient in every circumstance and situation. I decided to be better rather than bitter. That one choice has made a world of difference in my life. To God be the glory. Praise God.

And if it seem evil unto you to serve the Lord, choose you this day whom ye will serve; whether the gods which your fathers served that were on the other side of the flood, or the gods of the Amorites, in whose land ye dwell: but as for me and my house, we will serve the Lord.

(Joshua 24:15)

Chapter 6:
Have an Exit Strategy

"Exit strategy" is a term used to denote a means of leaving a current situation. In business, it is defined as transition management. Transition management is the declaration or plan to move from one phase to another (e.g., change in ownership or operations). The key emphasis of an exit strategy is on devising a plan of exit. Pastor John Hagee says it best: 100 percent of living beings die. There are, however, few exceptions to the death rule (e.g., Enoch).

And Enoch walked with God: and he was not; for God took him.
Genesis 5:24

Preparation for the transition from this mortal life to eternal life is imperative. Regardless of whether you believe in heaven, hell, or neither, we are destined to spend eternity somewhere. The lack of belief in heaven is a choice. It is an indication of belief in an alternative, named or not. It does not matter what the alternative state is; it is an indication that something else reigns as true in the subconscious. It is our right to hold fast to what we believe, and regardless of that belief, we get to the next state via death. An exit strategy should be formulated according to our beliefs. Do not be deceived; the choices made during the course of life affect us afterward. There are many opinions on the matter. No matter the differences in the opinions, one thing is common; each of us, through our choices in life, make decisions—intentional or unintentional—regarding where we will spend eternity.

Jesus answered and said unto him, Verily, verily, I say unto thee,
Except a man be born again, he cannot see the kingdom of God.
John 3:3

We plan for retirement. We plan to buy a house. We plan where we will go for summer vacations. We remain silent and uncertain, however, about where we will spend eternity. If it were not so sad, it would be comical. Life is to be enjoyed, but it is not the end. God gave us his son so that we can live the more abundant life here on earth. Yet no matter how good or hard this life is, it is only a dress rehearsal for eternity. In the totality of the matter, this vapor called life is not the final destination. We get a say in our final destination and should be planning for it.

The Lord rewarded me according to my righteousness: according to
the cleanness of my hands hath he recompensed me. For I have kept
the ways of the Lord, and have not wickedly departed from my God.
For all his judgments were before me: and as for his statutes, I did
not depart from them. I was also upright before him, and have kept
myself from mine iniquity. Therefore the Lord hath recompensed me
according to my righteousness; according to
my cleanness in his eyesight.
II Samuel 22:21-25

Never in my worst nightmare did I ever think that one of my children would precede me in death. It is a reminder that life is short, and we do not know the day or the hour we will leave it. Plan where you will spend eternity. It cannot be by happenstance or accident. Life's ultimate goal is to spend eternity with God and our family members who have died in Christ.

And regarding the question, friends, that has come up about what
happens to those already dead and buried, we don't want you in the

dark any longer. First off, you must not carry on over them like people who have nothing to look forward to, as if the grave were the last word. Since Jesus died and broke loose from the grave, God will most certainly bring back to life those who died in Jesus.

And then this: We can tell you with complete confidence—we have the Master's word on it—that when the Master comes again to get us, those of us who are still alive will not get a jump on the dead and leave them behind. In actual fact, they'll be ahead of us. The Master himself will give the command. Archangel thunder! God's trumpet blast! He'll come down from heaven and the dead in Christ will rise—they'll go first. Then the rest of us who are still alive at the time will be caught up with them into the clouds to meet the Master. Oh, we'll be walking on air! And then there will be one huge family reunion with the Master. So reassure one another with these words.

I Thessalonians 4: 13-18 (The Message Bible)

Exit Strategy Checklist:

Yes/No	Have you accepted Jesus as Lord and Savior?
Yes/No	Do you love God and others?
Yes/No	Do you seek God's wisdom to make decisions?
Yes/No	Do you live in the fear of God, seeking to please him (virtuous living)?

Answering yes to the above questions is the way to devise and develop your strategy for departing this life. It is imperative that you know absolutely where you will spend eternity. There are no second chances to get it right. According to Paul in Romans 1, many will make choices contrary to God's will.

For I am not ashamed of the Gospel (good news) of Christ, for it is God's power working unto salvation [for deliverance from eternal

*death] to everyone who believes with a personal trust
and a confident surrender and firm reliance, to the Jew first
and also to the Greek,*
*For in the Gospel a righteousness which God ascribes is revealed, both
springing from faith and leading to faith [disclosed through the way
of faith that arouses to more faith]. As it is written, The man who
through faith is just and upright shall live and
shall live by faith.*
*For God's [holy] wrath and indignation are revealed from heaven
against all ungodliness and unrighteousness of men, who in their
wickedness repress and hinder the truth and make it inoperative.
For that which is known about God is evident to them and made
plain in their inner consciousness, because God [himself]
has shown it to them.*
*For ever since the creation of the world his invisible nature and
attributes, that is, his eternal power and divinity, have been made
intelligible and clearly discernible in and through the things that have
been made (his handiworks). So [men] are without excuse [altogether
without any defense or justification],*
*Because when they knew and recognized him as God, they did not
honor and glorify him as God or give him thanks. But instead they
became futile and godless in their thinking [with vain imaginings,
foolish reasoning, and stupid speculations] and their
senseless minds were darkened.*
*Claiming to be wise, they became fools [professing to be smart, they
made simpletons of themselves].*
*And by them the glory and majesty and excellence of the immortal
God were exchanged for and represented by images, resembling mortal
man and birds and beasts and reptiles.*
***Therefore God gave them up in the lusts of their [own] hearts** to
sexual impurity, to the dishonoring of their bodies among themselves
[abandoning them to the degrading power of sin],*
*Because they exchanged the truth of God for a lie and worshiped and
served the creature rather than the Creator, Who is blessed forever!
Amen (so be it).*

*For this reason God gave them over and abandoned them to vile
affections and degrading passions. For their women exchanged their
natural function for an unnatural and abnormal one,
And the men also turned from natural relations with women and were
set ablaze (burning out, consumed) with lust for one another—men
committing shameful acts with men and suffering in their own bodies
and personalities the inevitable consequences and penalty of their
wrong-doing and going astray,
which was [their] fitting retribution.
And so, since they did not see fit to acknowledge God or approve of
him or consider him worth the knowing, God gave them over to a base
and condemned mind to do things not proper
or decent but loathsome,
Until they were filled (permeated and saturated) with every kind of
unrighteousness, iniquity, grasping and covetous greed, and malice.
[They were] full of envy and jealousy, murder, strife, deceit and
treachery, ill will and cruel ways. [They were] secret
backbiters and gossipers,
Slanderers, hateful to and hating God, full of insolence, arrogance,
[and] boasting; inventors of new forms of evil, disobedient
and undutiful to parents.
[They were] without understanding, conscienceless and faithless,
heartless and loveless [and] merciless.
Though they are fully aware of God's righteous decree that those who
do such things deserve to die, they not only do them themselves but
approve and applaud others who practice them.*
Romans 1:16-32 (Amplified Bible)

Choose well. The exit strategy is developed through the sum of life
choices.

Wherefore they are no more twain, but one flesh. What therefore God hath joined together, let not man put asunder.

(Matthew 19:6)

CHAPTER 7:
Special Essay: Covenant Breaker

There is a minister at my local church, Rev. Matthew Bereal, who always says, "For best results, follow the directions." I have learned over the years he is right. The covenant—the promise—is holy to God. When a man and a woman make the vow of holy matrimony, it pleases God. The institution of marriage did not originate with man but with God. The idea of family is God's. It is a precious gift to mankind. We all live with a desire to be part of something bigger than ourselves. What can be more important than family? The entire concept of family originates from the loving relationship of a Father for a son. The love for the son caused the Father to see his son's need and provide for that specific need.

And the Lord God said, It is not good that the man should be alone;
I will make him an help meet for him.
Genesis 2:18

God says it is not good to be alone. He made the choice to present to Adam in the Garden of Eden a beautiful helpmeet to accomplish and share in all the excitement that life in the Garden of Eden offered. God, who is the giver of every good and perfect gift, according to Scripture, created her to perfection. God provided for Adam a perfect dwelling. Adam himself was a perfect specimen, made in the image of the Almighty

> **God hates divorce**

God. Adam's responsibility was a perfect passion. I have no doubt that the woman brought forth by the hands of God from the rib of Adam was nothing less than perfect, as were all God's prior creations. She was made especially for the husband for whom God had created her. When Adam looked upon her, an expression of desire and praise broke forth from his mouth.

And Adam said, This is now bone of my bones, and flesh of my flesh: she shall be called Woman, because she was taken out of Man.
Genesis 2:23

What a wonderful beginning. Yet today, somehow the marriage covenant has become perverted and shunned. Statistics state that over 51 percent of heterosexual Christian marriages in America result in divorce. How can this be?

Great peace have they which love thy law: and nothing shall offend them.
Psalm 119:165

Great peace is the result of obedience. For best results in our marriages and families, we have to discipline ourselves to follow God's directions.

God's direction for the husband is as follows:

So ought men to love their wives as their own bodies. He that loveth his wife loveth himself. For no man ever yet hated his own flesh; but nourisheth and cherisheth it, even as the Lord the church:
Ephesians 5:28,29

Husbands, go all out in your love for your wives, exactly as Christ did for the church—a love marked by giving, not getting. Christ's love makes the church whole. His words evoke her beauty. Everything he does and says is designed to bring the best out of her, dressing her in dazzling white silk, radiant with holiness. And that is how

husbands ought to love their wives. They're really doing themselves a
favor—since they're already "one" in marriage.
Ephesians 5:25-28 (The Message Bible)

God's direction for the wife is as follows::

Wives, understand and support your husbands in ways that show your
support for Christ. The husband provides leadership to his wife the
way Christ does to his church, not by domineering but by cherishing.
So just as the church submits to Christ as he exercises such leadership,
wives should likewise submit to their husbands.
Ephesians 5:22-24 (The Message Bible)

That they may teach the young women to be sober, to love their
husbands, to love their children, To be discreet, chaste, keepers at
home, good, obedient to their own husbands, that the word of God be
not blasphemed.
Titus 2:4-5

God's direction for the children is as follows:

Children, obey your parents in the Lord: for this is right.
Honor thy father and mother; which is the first
commandment with promise;
That it may be well with thee, and thou mayest live long
on the earth.
Ephesians 6:1-3

God's directions are clear and precise and are non-negotiable.
Marriage is important to God. It is because marriage is so important
to God that the marriage design is being attacked from all sides.
Society is trying to redefine marriage. God defines marriage as a
covenant between God, a man, and a woman. The family home as
the basic teaching apparatus, where our children can observe healthy
love between a man and a woman is being destroyed. The mirrored

reflection of a husband loving his wife and a wife honoring and respecting her husband is being broken in far too many homes today. Yet God's word on the matter is unchanged. God is unrepentant in his expectations of the marriage covenant.

Now these are the commandments, the statutes, and the judgments, which the Lord your God commanded to teach you, that ye might do them in the land whither ye go to possess it:
That thou mightest fear the Lord thy God, to keep all his statutes and his commandments, which I command thee, thou, and thy son, and thy son's son, all the days of thy life; and that thy days may be prolonged.
Hear therefore, O Israel, and observe to do it; that it may be well with thee, and that ye may increase mightily, as the Lord God of thy fathers hath promised thee, in the land that floweth with milk and honey.
Hear, O Israel: The Lord our God is one Lord:
And thou shalt love the Lord thy God with all thine heart, and with all thy soul, and with all thy might.
And these words, which I command thee this day, shall be in thine heart:
And thou shalt teach them diligently unto thy children, and shalt talk of them when thou sittest in thine house, and when thou walkest by the way, and when thou liest down, and when thou risest up.
Deuteronomy 6:1-7

Our marriages are worth fighting for. When we allow our marriages to disintegrate before our eyes, and we sit complacently, waiting for the other person to change, we break our covenant with God and surrender our will to another. It is God's will that none of our dreams and desires go unfulfilled. That includes the desire of men and women to live in an atmosphere of love and sufficiency. We complicate matters by trying to define our own directions. This new definition causes us to submit to our lusts. It is those lusts that oppose the will of God in our lives. I say to you: stop it; just simply stop it.

How do we simply *stop* the decay of our marriages? We discipline ourselves. Hear me—I did not say we discipline our spouse. We hold ourselves accountable to our role and responsibilities in the marriage. Self-discipline is key in marriage. The will has to be set that divorce is not an option. The decision must be made by the two who are now one flesh that I will walk in my God-ordained office (my role as husband or wife), obey what God has commanded of me in this office (ministry), and wait for the manifestation of God's healing for my marriage. My confession for my spouse every day is my love for him. I say about my marriage what God says about my marriage, in spite of its reality. I keep confessing God's will for my marriage and walking in my defined role until I see the change for which I am waiting.

> **There is simplicity in Christ**

I fear, lest by any means, as the serpent beguiled Eve through his subtlety, so your minds should be corrupted from the simplicity that is in Christ.
2 Corinthians 11:3

It is so simple, yet we make it hard. It is the same principle exercised in the receipt of salvation. We receive salvation by faith in God. It is the same for every promise of God. It is impossible to please God without faith. Every promise is obtained through faith. The healing of marriages is obtained through faith—never giving up; never conceding to defeat; never, ever throwing in the towel. The key to success in marriage is to never give up or give out. For best results, follow the directions established by God for marriage.

*If a man vow a vow unto the Lord, or swear an oath to bind his soul
with a bond; he shall not break his word, he shall do according to all
that proceedeth out of his mouth.*
Numbers 30:2

In the matter of the marriage covenant, what does God say?

*And here's a second offense: You fill the place of worship with your
whining and sniveling because you don't get what you want from
God. Do you know why? Simple. Because God was there as a witness
when you spoke your marriage vows to your young bride, and now
you've broken those vows, broken the faith-bond with your vowed
companion, your covenant wife. God, not you, made marriage. His
Spirit inhabits even the smallest details of marriage. And what does he
want from marriage? Children of God, that's what. So guard the spirit
of marriage within you.
Don't cheat on your spouse.*
*"I hate divorce," says the God of Israel. God-of-the-Angel-Armies says,
"I hate the violent dismembering of the 'one flesh' of marriage." So
watch yourselves. Don't let your guard down. Don't cheat.*
Malachi 2:13-16 (The Message Bible)

*He answered, "Haven't you read in your Bible that the Creator
originally made man and woman for each other, male and female?
And because of this, a man leaves father and mother and is firmly
bonded to his wife, becoming one flesh—no longer two bodies but one.
Because God created this organic union of the two sexes, no one should
desecrate his art by cutting them apart."*
Matthew 19:4-6 (The Message Bible)

The marriage vow is sacred unto God. Keep it, protect it, and honor
it.

But the end of all things is at hand: be ye therefore sober, and watch unto prayer.

(1 Peter 4:7)

Chapter 8:
Last Words: The Tipping Point

Situation awareness is the perception of environmental elements with respect to time and/or space, the comprehension of their meaning, and the projection of their status after some variable has changed, such as time. Situation awareness involves being attentive to what is happening in our vicinity, so that we can understand how information, events, and our own actions will impact goals and objectives, both immediately and in the near future.[1] Situation awareness is simply watching and responding accordingly for best results.

There are three major aspects to situation awareness for our purposes:

- Knowing the enemy and his obsession
- Being aware of the end time and where we are today, relative to it
- Knowing the devil's plan for mankind

Who is the real enemy? It is not people.

Be sober, be vigilant; because your adversary the devil, as a roaring lion, walketh about, seeking whom he may devour.
1 Peter 5:8

---

[1]   Wikipedia

What is the real enemy's obsession? It is not your material things.

The thief cometh not, but for to steal, and to kill, and to destroy.
John 10:10a

Note: The devil, the roaring lion, and the thief are one and the same. He comes to steal the Word of God from your heart, to kill God's perfect will for you, and to destroy your claim to an abundant life on earth and everlasting life in eternity.

When is the end-time? It is not calculated or predictable, according to humanity's clock.

For man also knoweth not his time: as the fishes that are taken in an evil net, and as the birds that are caught in the snare; so are the sons of men snared in an evil time, when it falleth suddenly upon them.
Ecclesiastes 9:12

Where are we, relative to the end time? Only God knows for certain.

But thou, O Daniel, shut up the words, and seal the book, even to the time of the end: many shall run to and fro, and knowledge shall be increased
Daniel 12:4

And he said, go thy way, Daniel: for the words are closed up and sealed till the time of the end.
Daniel 12:9

" 'Go on about your business, Daniel,' he said. 'The message is confidential and under lock and key until the end, until things are about to be wrapped up. The populace will be washed clean and made like new. But the wicked will just keep on being wicked, without a

*clue about what is happening. Those who live wisely and well will
understand what's going on.'*
Daniel 12:9-10 (The Message Bible)

What is the devil's plan for mankind? Hell.

*And whosoever was not found written in the book of life
was cast into the lake of fire.*
Revelation 20:15

Note: The devil's plan is to take as many as possible with him to
hell.

We should have a response to the devil's plan. Our responses are
to repent and forsake all sin. Mankind's greatest challenge today
is continuing in love for one another and repenting and forsaking
when we mistakenly do not love one another.

*Owe no man any thing, but to love one another: for he that loveth
another hath fulfilled the law.*
Romans 13:8

Regardless of circumstance, situation, test, or trial, the greatest
challenge we face is to love one another as ourselves. As we experience
personal hardship and disappointment, we tend to blame others. We
lose our ability to see each other through God's eyes of love. Then
we justify or rationalize our mistreatment and hateful ways toward
others. When love ceases to flow freely, we find ourselves fearful,
unbelieving, or practicing abominable things, such as murder,
whoremongering, sorcery, idolatry, and lying.

Afterward, we do not repent because we feel the targets of our wrath
deserve the abuse or mistreatment. The end result is that the real
enemy wins. Our ultimate goal, according to Scripture, is to love.

Master, which is the great commandment in the law?

Jesus said unto him, thou shalt love the Lord thy God with all thy
heart, and with all thy soul, and with all thy mind.
This is the first and great commandment.
And the second is like unto it, thou shalt love thy neighbor as thyself.
On these two commandments hang all the law and the prophets.
Matthew 22:36-40

Malcolm Gladwell's book *The Tipping Point: How Little Things Can Make a Big Difference*, published in 2000, defines a tipping point as "the moment of critical mass, the threshold, the boiling point." The book describes the way in which small, everyday choices, decisions, and changes mark and alter our everyday lives. My son's death, though not a small occurrence in my life, was my tipping point. It was the moment that I—as well as my family—made significant decisions. We were faced with the impossible choice of being better or bitter about Jonathan's death. We wanted with all our hearts to be better, but the pain, agony, and sheer senselessness of Jonathan's death made it so much easier to hate and be full of bitterness. We had to make some hard choices and decisions during a time of extreme mental, emotional, and physical weakness and self-pity. These hard choices could not be put off, and we alone had to make them.

We made some of the decisions as individuals; others, we decided collectively as a family. For example, I had an uneasy feeling as I watched Jonathan back out of the driveway and head back to campus to complete his last semester at Clark Atlanta University. He was excited to take the journey again. As he drove away, I walked down the driveway's incline to watch him turn the corner of our street. I wished desperately that I had said more to him, but I didn't know what to say. We had prayed for traveling grace and asked God's angels to accompany him. I reminded him to drive the speed limit, and we said I love you to one another more than once. We gave each other hugs and kisses quickly as he jumped into the car. I reminded him to put on his seatbelt. We had said everything that needed saying, yet I felt as if I had left something unsaid. I started to stop him and hang on to him with one last, long, lingering hug, but I didn't. After Jonathan's death, I made a personal decision to acknowledge my feelings and make sure I hugged a little longer and a little tighter and say words of kindness whenever I got the chance. Never again will I regret not hugging a loved one as long and as tight as I can.

We made some collective decisions. My husband and I sat down after the funeral and talked about the grief process ahead of us. We made a commitment to one another that we would grieve together, no matter how long it took or how hard it got. We committed to counting on each other during the difficult times that were sure to come, and we agreed never to apologize to one another for missing our son. We call them our moments. We'll say, "I'm having a moment." It was our code that we needed to hold on to one another a little longer or a bit tighter. We agreed we would talk about him often and remember him at every family function from that time on. We made a vow to one another that we would come through this together.

We made decisions as a family, both our immediate and extended family. To honor Jonathan's memory, my mom established a foundation to provide scholarships to young people in our family to help with college expenses. It was our way of ensuring that generations forward would know about this terrific young man and his love for learning and education. Jonathan would encourage family and friends to give college a try, no matter what. He often told the story about his high school counselor, who told him he was not college material and that he should look into entering a trade school. That conversation became the real catalyst for Jonathan's pursuit of higher education. He always said, "How dare someone be so negative when he is supposed to be encouraging young people to reach and want more." Jonathan said that if our family had not told him that he could be and do anything he wanted in life, he might have believed that counselor. Instead, the counselor's words became the challenge that propelled Jonathan to want to succeed.

We made a decision as a family never to allow Jonathan's dreams to be silenced. We would speak for him everywhere we could.

We made many other decisions after Jonathan's death, and we have vowed to continue with them all. We use to talk about how we lost Jonathan until a friend reminded us that we did not "lose" him. She told us, "You know exactly where he is." She was right. I do know exactly where he is, and I know that I will see him again.

We are a family dwelling in the land of Goshen. Every provision has been made for us, as a family, to bloom where we are planted just like Israel's family. Regardless of the obstacles, problems, economy, or challenges, we know the formula for dwelling in the land of Goshen.

Step 1: Love God (fear and obey him)
Step 2: Seek wisdom
Step 3: Live virtuously

Let us hear the conclusion of the whole matter: Fear God, and keep his commandments: for this is the whole duty of man.
Ecclesiastes 12:13

Our Family

If my people, which are called by
my name, shall humble themselves,
and pray, and seek my face, and turn
from their wicked ways; then will I
hear from heaven, and will forgive
their sin, and will heal their land.

(2 Chronicles 7:14)

About the Author

Denise Kelley is an author, entrepreneur and highly sought-after speaker and teacher.

She attended college on a dual-degree scholarship program at Texas Southern and Rice Universities in Houston, Texas, where she studied computer science and electrical engineering.

Ms. Kelley is currently president and CEO of JK Technology, Inc., an engineering and information technology professional service staffing firm. She is the founder and president of ReGifts4u LLC, a web-based shopping experience (www.regifts4u.com).

Denise travels and speaks extensively throughout the United States, encouraging people to pursue their dreams with confidence.

Denise has been married for more than thirty-two years to her high school sweetheart, Joe. Together, they have three children—Joe II (Toni), Jonathan, and Brittany Blackman (Dominique)—and four grandchildren, Ashley, Halle, Kailyn, and Jonathan Bernard.